THE DUEL

Two Marksmen: One Battleground
KASHMIR

THE DUEL

Two Marksmen: One Battleground
KASHMIR

Ajay Singh

PENTAGON PRESS LLP

First published in 2025 by
PENTAGON PRESS LLP
206, Peacock Lane, Shahpur Jat
New Delhi-110049, India
Contact: 011-26490600

Typeset in Century Schoolbook, 11 Point
Printed at Aegean Offset Printers, Greater Noida

ISBN 978-81-988370-4-2

www.pentagonpress.in

For Monisha...

With whom I have lost every duel
we have had in all our years,

But still won everything.

Contents

Author's Note

The idea for this book actually came about almost three years ago – around mid-2022 or so – when I was driving through Kashmir with my friends, Raj Acharya and Ashit Ghelani. As the winding road took us through thickly wooden hills, with interspersed villages and the occasional army camp along they way, one of them said, "Just imagine, if one sniper is hidden on the hill out there. He can hit at will, and get away before anyone can even react." The conversation trailed along the subject of a marksman hiding in the undergrowth and the first glimmerings of a story began forming in my mind.

Like all stories, it germinated for months, if not years. In between, I visited Kashmir twice again – around the period of 2023-24, where the mood and the very psyche of the people was slowly changing. The shadow of terrorism was ebbing, peace was returning, and the locals were focused on more essential things like finding jobs and making a livelihood. In my conversations with locals and visits to towns and villages deep in the interior, I could feel the change. Some of the more seasoned Kashmiri watchers warned that it was too good to last. Pakistan would definitely want to ferment trouble once again. The prevailing environment of peace and normalcy did not suit their plans and they would definitely try to disrupt it.

With this came the idea of the Pakistani ISI sending a seasoned sniper into the valley to re-establish their sway.

He would create terror by eliminating police and military leaders and assassinating moderate politicians. The tourists thronging into Kashmir, also emerged as prime targets. In the book, the Pakistani terrorist Aurangzeb, deliberately kills innocents to make an impact. The book was written in 2024, and the tragic Pahalgam massacre took place in April 2025. Some of the events described in the story seemed to foreshadow that dastardly action.

This is the work of fiction, but actual locations and events have been used to heighten the realism. The book hopes to bring out the true face of terrorism in the valley and also highlights the rigours and trauma of all those who combat it. It also delves deep into the psyche of the ordinary Kashmiris who have faced the scourge of terrorism for decades, and have been its greatest victims.

The book has been through so many alliterations and refinements. It has evolved each time I narrated it and I am grateful to all who listened patiently, added so much to it, and helped it take on the form that it finally has. This story is as much theirs, as it is mine.

At the end of it all, I do hope you will enjoy the story. I hope the characters resonate in your minds, and that the beauty, charms and hidden dangers of the mountains and valleys of Kashmir come alive in these pages. And if you do put down the book with a faint gasp of surprise at the ending – that would be the icing on the cake.

And now, let me take you into the pages where you will meet the duellists, see the prize they both covet, and witness the deadly battle they wage in the beautiful battleground of Kashmir.

Ajay Singh

Major Characters

Captain Amar Rathore

A young Captain posted in Kashmir, who is an expert marksman and uses his skills to eliminate the terrorist network in his area. Mid-twenties, young, brash, courageous to the point of recklessness.

Major Aurangzeb

A Pakistani ISI Major who has over 70 kills to his name. He uses his rifle '*Badr*' to kill targets at incredibly long ranges. Early thirties; tall, light eyes – always wears a *Keffiyeh* around his face; only his eyes are visible.

Shazia Junaid

A Kashmiri school teacher who stays with her parents in a fairly remote house on the outskirts of the town. Her family has been afflicted by a great tragedy they can't get over. Both Amar and Aurangzeb vie for her attention. Extremely beautiful, with an air of vulnerability.

Tejpal

A local Kashmiri Pundit who is an undercover agent for the Army. One of Amar's most trusted informers. His family was hounded out of their village and now he takes great risks to fight the terrorists. He unfortunately takes one risk too many with tragic consequences.

Umar Husseini

The local politician of a moderate party, who genuinely wants to do good for his constituency, and hence is a prime target for the terrorists, especially during the campaigning for elections.

Dr. Mirwaiz

The local sympathizer who actively helps terrorists and shelters them in his home. He is the contact man between the ISI and the terrorists and supplies arms and ammunition to Aurangzeb and his group. He also treats injured terrorists.

Colonel Sangha

The no-nonsense Commanding Officer who has to keep his area safe and also curb Amar's impetuousness. A tall, grey-bearded Sikh officer with a rough manner that hides a caring and compassionate nature.

'Begum'

A mysterious burqa-clad woman who passes information to Aurangzeb, and helps him in his activities.

Abdul Chacha and Iqbal

A local tea shop owner whom Amar befriends. Iqbal is his nephew who has been blinded by police riot pellets and is angry and resentful. Amar tries to help him and even connects him to an eye specialist to recover his sight.

Sameer

Amar's devoted buddy who is by his side during the most dangerous missions.

Sajid and Majid

Two brothers who are part of Aurangzeb's *tanzeem* and act as his personal bodyguards. They are devoted to him, but he sacrifices them for his personal ends.

The House with the Blue Door

Night falls suddenly in Kashmir. In a matter of minutes, the sun-drenched meadows and hills lose their hues and take on shades of grey of the approaching night. The crisp air acquires a sharp bite, and people draw their *firhans* closer around them. Nightfall often brings with it an air of menace. It is a sense of danger that has hovered over Kashmir for almost two decades – ever since Pakistan-sponsored terrorism scourged this beautiful land – and the night holds many unseen dangers. Over the past few years, the spectre of terrorism has reduced considerably, but it has never quite gone away. And though the state has slowly returned to normalcy, danger always seems to lie just below the surface.

When night closed in on the outskirts of Sopore, the small town was still lively. Shops were open, and the streets were filled with people milling around, sipping *kahwa* in the innumerable roadside stalls. A wedding had just taken place and the sounds of traditional Kashmiri music, and the aroma of rice and meats wafted through the narrow streets. There was a time when the area of Sopore-Baramulla – a mountainous, heavily wooded area, just 30 kilometres from the Line of Control which separated it from Pakistan Occupied Kashmir – was a hotbed of terrorism. Terrorists could infiltrate into the area with ease from the other side, find sanctuary in the hills, and simply disappear into anonymity. But, like much of Kashmir in the early 2020s or so, the area was returning to normalcy. The sounds of music and the bright lights showed that much of the dark days had indeed been pushed away but had not completely disappeared gone. Check posts still dotted the crossroads and junctions, where tense-looking security men peered out through sand-bagged bunkers, rifles in hand. Army and police patrols drove past frequently, keeping an eye out for any suspicious activity. That vigilance could never really stop but there seemed to be a greater sense of rapport between the security men and the locals. The tension that once cut like a knife through the air now seemed to have reduced considerably, at least overtly.

Some distance from the town, a young army officer paced around in his camp. It was a typical camp, held by a company commanded by Captain Amar Rathore set up on the outskirts of the town. The camp, like all other installations, was heavily fortified and surrounded with layers of barbed wire and barricades. Entry was restricted to the main gate and a smaller one in the rear, and watchtowers and searchlights dotted the perimeter. These camps were usually set up in their areas of responsibility from where troops could observe and control the area and move out to conduct anti-terrorist operations or just patrol the area. It was a lonely, dangerous life for the men there – especially when they were out on operations – with unseen dangers and the knowledge that each moment could potentially be their last.

Amar walked around the camp impatiently. He was wearing a bulletproof jacket and *patka* – which most soldiers donned during operations. In his hands, he held a Kalashnikov 7.62 sniper rifle. It was longer and heavier than the standard issue INSAS rifles carried by most soldiers, and was a specialist weapon designed to fire at long ranges with great accuracy. His team of soldiers, all armed and dressed in protective gear, were standing close by. Like Amar, they too were tense and ready, awaiting a signal..

Amar's mobile phone buzzed, and he grabbed it immediately. A WhatsApp message appeared. It came from an unknown number – Amar had deliberately not saved it with a name – and though the number kept changing, he knew it by heart. It was from his most trusted informer, Tejpal, and the message showed just an emoji of a handshake. He had been waiting for that message for days and knew what it meant. Almost instantly, he waved to his men, and galvanized them into action. No words were said; they moved out in small groups on foot, leaving from a small gate in the rear of the camp. As they moved out unseen, two vehicles emerged from the main gate, entered the main road that passed alongside it, and sped away in the opposite direction. They moved without headlights, but their movement was detected – as it was designed to. From the road outside, a man in a large *firhan* took out his mobile and whispered, "Two vehicles moving towards Sonamarg road."

Amar led his men on foot, moving rapidly but silently. Their own move had not been seen and he hoped he would surprise his target when he reached their objective. Two other small parties, led by a junior commissioned officer (JCO) each, were also headed for the same location, coming in from another direction to avoid detection. Amar had coordinated the move of the different parties expertly, as they linked up in the vicinity of the village where the terrorists were reported to be hiding.

They approached a rather remote hamlet at the base of a heavily wooded hillock, keeping to the side of the single track leading to it. As they neared it, a Bakharwal shepherd passed by, followed by his sheep dog and a line of sheep. Amar did not try to hide from him, but deliberately allowed him to come closer. As the shepherd passed Amar, he asked, *"Janaab, jara paani milega?"* (Could I have some water?) Amar pulled out his water bottle and poured some into his outstretched palms. As he bent to drink, the shepherd whispered imperceptibly, *"Teesri galli, chautha ghar, neela darwaza, teen."*(The third lane, fourth house, with the blue door. Three of them.)

The shepherd was 'Joker', Amar's most trusted informant. He had never been wrong in his information earlier, and if he was right this time too, they would hit the jackpot. The shepherd disappeared into the distance, his flock following him, and Amar and his party broke into a run towards the small hamlet, whose lights could be seen twinkling just a short distance away.

About a kilometre or so from the village, they linked up with a police party, led by SP Altaf Ali. They shook hands with warmth. Altaf was a highly respected police officer of Sopore. The two men had gone through a lot together and had been largely instrumental in clearing the area of terrorists who once infested the town and the forests around it. They had shared dangers and experienced close shaves together and greatly respected each other. They hid in the shadows and spoke in whispers as their men fanned out in the woods surrounding the village.

"Captain *Saab*, are you sure your intelligence is correct."

"Yes, it is. Joker has never been wrong. They are hiding in that village."

SP Altaf looked worried, "Yes, but are you sure. If we go into the wrong house, it could cause trouble."

Amar nodded, "I am definite. He says there are three terrorists in that house." He pointed to the one with a blue door, which Joker had indicated. "We have to close in without being detected. If they are who I think they are, they will be heavily armed."

The men fanned out. They knew the drill; they had done it dozens of times before. The army would lay an outer cordon around the village, and an inner cordon around the target house. They would then close in along with the police who would help identify known militants. It was a dangerous and delicate operation. At any stage, the hidden militants could open fire. And if the attackers were detected before the cordon was in place, they would just slip away under cover of the darkness.

Amar called out to the JCOs who would be establishing the cordons. They were both seasoned and trusted men, and could be banked upon. They had practised and rehearsed the operation many times and each man knew what had to be done. He whispered out the orders.

"Ranjit Saab, inner cordon *lagayiye*; Om Prakash, the outer one." He turned to Altaf, "I will need some of your men with each of my parties. I will move in and try to flush the terrorists out."

The parties took up their positions. Amar moved through the dark narrow streets at the head of a small column. His heart was pounding with the adrenal fuelled tension that rose at the start of each operation. Just then, a dog started barking.

The men froze where they were. It was the worst damn thing. The barking dogs could give them away and alert the terrorists, if they were really hiding in the house.

Inside, behind the blue door, three men were eating at a table in a darkened room when they heard the barking. The glow of a solitary candle illuminated the room. They paused eating as the barking became louder. A slightly elderly man, who seemed to be the owner of the house, walked towards the door, looking worried. An armed man peered through the curtains, hoping to see something.

The dog barked again. It was a large mastiff tied to the porch, and its barking became even more frantic as the soldiers closed in towards the house.

In the street outside, the soldiers froze. Then slowly, they resumed their action, as JCO Ranjit Singh led his party forward cautiously. Amar went nearer trying to gauge the situation. He looked around for a suitable position for himself, and then pointed towards a low house close by. He moved there silently, accompanied by his buddy, Sameer. They had been together for almost a year now, and had participated in over a dozen operations. They had reached a stage of understanding where they did not need words to convey what was to be done. They clambered on to the roof, and took position behind a low parapet from where the house with the blue door was in their sights. Amar carefully selected a position and set up his sniper rifle on a bipod there. Then he fitted his sniper scope – complete with a night vision device – and scanned the area. Focussing on the target and its darkened windows, he could see nothing behind them,

In the room, the elderly man hurriedly snuffed out the candle. "I don't feel good about this."

The leader picked up his weapon, "Did your informer mention any activity from the army camp?"

"He said two vehicles had gone on the Sonamarg Road, nothing else. No activity in our direction. But that could be a trick. Come on, you had better hide."

Another terrorist picked up his weapon and stood by the window. The elderly man led the two main leaders towards a hidden trapdoor in the rear of the house, opened it, and guided them out.

The dog barked again. JCO Ranjit Singh's presence had alerted it. He jerked back, but his movement was seen by the terrorist at the window.

He shouted out, "Army dogs have come." He cocked his AK-56 and pointed it towards the approaching JCO, but even as he did so, a single shot rang out, hit him on the side of his temple; he slumped dead to the floor.

The shot had come from Amar's rifle. The terrorist had exposed himself for just a few seconds, but that was enough; Amar had downed him with just one shot before he could fire at the JCO.

As Ranjit Singh and his men crouched around the house, another burst of fire came from within. The second terrorist had fired to keep them at bay.

Amar continued watching the window of the darkened house through his sniper scope. His night vision was on, and through its ghostly greenish glow, he could see movement within. He radioed Ranjit, "Don't go closer. There are two or three more inside. Wait."

He watched even as the terrorist inside fired short bursts, rushing from one window to another, changing position constantly and keeping firing. None of the soldiers returned the fire. They had obviously rehearsed this situation and knew what had to be done.

Amar nodded to Sameer, who let off a short burst towards the window from where the firing had last come. Amar watched through his scope, and fired at the adjoining window.

As Sameer's bullets crashed into the window, the terrorist lifted his weapon above his head and while still under cover, let loose a burst of random fire. He then rushed to the next window, thrust his barrel out to fire, and exposed himself for less than two seconds; a single shot from Amar felled him.

The firing stopped and a deathly quiet prevailed. The dogs had stopped barking. The elderly man had led the other two terrorists out through a hidden trapdoor and a narrow tunnel emerging in the forest almost 200 yards away. He was panting with fear and exertion; his body was soaked in sweat. His two companions seemed to handle themselves better. They were young and tough, their bodies hardened by years of constant strife.

Amar continued scanning the windows, one at a time. He knew he had hit the terrorists, but did not know if they were alive or dead, or whether there were any more inside. He waited for a long time, and seeing no activity inside, radioed the JCO, "Ranjit, search party *andar* le chalo."

Ranjit nodded. This was the most dangerous part of the job –entry into an unknown house. He and three others approached cautiously, taking positions on both sides of the door. He muttered a prayer, took a deep breath, and kicked the door open, firing two short bursts as he rushed in. The other two followed and slowly looked around the room. When their eyes got used to the dark, they made out the two dead terrorists, lying next to the windows where they had been hit. On the floor above, a woman started wailing. Slowly, the other soldiers entered, and room by room, they searched the house, till they homed in on the cellar and discovered the trapdoor leading to the tunnel.

He reported on the radio, "*Saab*. Two dead terrorists. And we found a tunnel leading outside."

Amar: "Damn. They must have escaped through it. The tunnel could not be very long."

He asked the outer cordon, "Sarv Lal, any activity your side?"

"No Sir. My cordon is in place. No one has come this side."

Amar tried to figure out where the escapees could have gone. "They will try to cross the LOC. They will be heading in that direction."

He scanned the area through his sniper scope, focusing on the heavily wooded hills in the adjoining area. He saw only dense foliage. Sameer too scanned the area with his own night vision binoculars. In the darkness beyond, the elderly man along with his two companions emerged from a deep grove in the forest, the old man panting from the exertion.

The leader hissed, "Stop that noise. The Indians will hear us. We have to get away from here. The LOC is just three kilometres away. We have to reach it quickly." He took the lead and began running in the direction of the LOC, followed by the other terrorist. The old man went after them breathing heavily. He was not a terrorist, just a sympathizer and his movement was not so fast or fluid, nor could he keep under cover.

It was Sameer who detected his movement and trained his binoculars in that direction, "*Saab,* there." He pointed to a bush at the edge of the grove, and Amar aimed his rifle at it. Through his scope, he too had seen the movement, and had made out someone there.

Amar focused on the figure, and adjusted his aiming mark, "Range 585, wind speed two knots left to right," he whispered to himself, and adjusted the rifle sight. Just then, the elderly man appeared momentarily, and Amar fired; his bullet struck the base of his neck killing him instantly.

At the sound of the shot, the terrorist in front of him turned and fired. That was a mistake. The flash gave away his position and Amar saw what he had been looking for. He adjusted his aiming mark, and waited for another tell-tale blink of fire. Another staccato of fire came just a moment later, and Amar fired, hitting the terrorist in the chest and hurtling him backwards.

The leading terrorist was around forty yards ahead of the others. He continued running even as the firing continued behind him. He was obviously more experienced than the others and did not fire back. Rather, he changed direction and crawled towards a small nullah, using its low banks for cover. He pulled a grenade from his *firhan* and prepared to hurl it when the Indian soldiers come close. Across the crest line was the LOC, and beyond it lay the safety of Pakistan and his handlers. He had to get there somehow. He could hear the crunch of Pakistani artillery fire as they opened up, to cover his own movements. It was standard practice. The Pakistanis always provided covering fire for their terrorists. He crawled up slowly. If he could get across the crest line, he would be able to reach safety.

Amar and Sameer continued observing the scene from their positions. They were too seasoned not to go rushing ahead, even though they knew they had at least two confirmed hits. There would be other terrorists there as well, waiting for them to come close. Or perhaps that terrorist would make a dash for the LOC. Amar put himself in the mind of the terrorist, and then, shifted his scope a little beyond, aiming at a spot, just below the crest line. That would be where the terrorist would emerge to get across. It was a good 600 yards away, and he would have just around two seconds to make the shot.

He focused his aim at that spot, slowed down his breathing till he was deadly still, and seemed to be carved in stone, as he continued watching, unblinking.

From the top of the nullah, just a few yards from where Amar was aiming, the terrorist emerged. At first, only the top of his *mast gul* cap was visible. He had to make one leap across the nullah to reach safety. He crouched and jumped; Amar's bullet struck him in mid-air, and hurled him sideways to the ground.

Sameer whooped, "Sir, you got him!"

He half arose, when Amar grabbed him and pulled him down roughly, "You fool. Don't move till you are sure your enemy is dead."

They scanned the area, and waited as the other soldiers and police joined them, and then began moving cautiously ahead. They crossed the body of the elderly man – the sympathizer – and a little beyond that, the other terrorist;

turning them both over to make sure they were dead. Then they moved ahead towards the third terrorist, whose body lay just below the crest of the ridge.

SP Altaf had also closed in and joined Amar as they carefully approached the body. The terrorist was obviously dead, but they still observed it for a good ten minutes before going up to it. Amar turned the body on its back, revealing a bloodied face with a neat wound on one temple.

Altaf looked the body and slapped Amar on his back, "Well, well, well ...! Guess who we got. Ghazi himself."

Captain Amar Rathore and his men returned to their camp late the next day, after winding down the operation, handing over the bodies to the police and completing the numerous formalities and documentation. He was exhausted as he walked into his operations room, but in the exhilaration of the success, he didn't even feel it. He removed his *patka* and placed his rifle carefully at one side. Then he walked to a board headlined 'MILITANT ORGANISATION: SOPORE – BARAMULLA.' It contained photos of around 12 militants with a small write-up below each of them. Most had a red X across them, except for four. He picked up a red marker pen and crossed the remaining faces, one by one, till he came to Ghazi's photo, at the head of the organizational structure. He smiled, "Okay, you bastards. By now you must have found out that there are no 72 virgins waiting for you, right." He crossed out the photo with great relish and smiled "Let me see anyone else try to come to this area now."

Aurangzeb Enters Kashmir

On the other side of the Line of Control, in the Pakistani ISI headquarters, a Pakistani officer received a radio intercept. He listened with a worried expression and then walked into the officer of the commander, Colonel Rashid.

"Sir, There is some bad news. Ghazi, along with Afzal, Masood and Habibullah, embraced *shahadat* yesterday. They were killed in a raid just outside Sopore."

Colonel Rashid looked up, startled, "What? But why weren't they to be pulled back across the LOC?"

"Sir, we were in the process of doing it. In fact, they were in the safe house of Wani, when the raid took place. They were to have crossed the LOC tonight."

"What do we have in the area now?"

The staff officer looked a little worried, "None, Sir. Ghazi's *tanzeem* had lost eleven members in the past eight months. Ghazi was to have come back to raise another *tanzeem* which he could take back when this happened. We have nothing there now."

"Damn it. Sopore was totally under our control. It was our area. We could do what we liked there and even the security dogs dared not enter it. We have to regain our control over it. But why are the local militants quiet?"

"Sir, Things seem to have changed there. We no longer get the support we did earlier. Tourists are coming in now and new businesses opening up. The local boys are finding jobs and we are not even able to recruit them any longer."

The colonel's face clouded, "We have to raise another *tanzeem* there, and get control of the area once again. And I know just the man for it. Get me Major Aurangzeb."

II

Colonel Rashid was working in his office a few weeks later – a large map of Kashmir on the wall behind him – when a tall, well-built figure walked in. His face was covered by a checked black and white *keffiyeh* scarf, which he habitually wore, with a flat woollen cap – called the *Mast Gul* cap – on his head. Between the cap and the scarf, his eyes peered out. They were cold and narrow, crinkled at the corners by years of squinting in the sun. They were the eyes of a man capable of great violence and wanton cruelty. A long rifle was slung over his shoulder, which he carried with easy nonchalance – almost as if the weapon was an extension of his body. He gave a half salute.

"*Salaam Aliekum, Janaab.*"

Colonel Rashid stood up and reached out to shake hands with obvious pleasure, "Major Aurangzeb. Back from Afghanistan at last. Your mission there was a great success. Congratulations."

"It was a long struggle there. And now the next target is...." He jabbed a finger on the map in the area of Srinagar.

Rashid continued, "That is why I have asked for you personally. We need you in Kashmir now. Things seem to have changed there. We no longer have the support we once did – especially after Article 370 was revoked. We have to give it another push. I want you to go here...," he traced the area of Baramula-Sopore with his finger. "Go there, start a *tanzeem*, instil fear and regain control of the area. That will be a start."

Aurangzeb looked at the map, "I know the area. I have operated in Kashmir before, and I know all about it." He slung his rifle off his shoulder and caressed the barrel, "This is my *Badr*, my sword. I have claimed over 70 infidels with it. *Badr* brings death without them even realizing where it came from." He pointed it towards the map, let the scope zoom in on the area of Sopore and pressed the trigger lightly. A dot of the laser designator came up on the map. "And I know about the art of fear. Don't worry, I will make them shiver at the name of Aurangzeb."

III

A few weeks later, Aurangzeb and around 10 -12 of his men crouched in a Pakistani army post on the line of control. They were all in *firhans* and Pathani suits and heavily armed. Aurangzeb was heavily cloaked, his face covered by the scarf he always wore. He watched across the line of control through his binoculars, seeing artillery fire falling with a soft clunk on the Indian side.

A Pakistani Captain, watching the firing beside him, put down his binoculars and said, "Our arty will be firing all night to keep the Indian heads down. It will ensure they don't leave their positions and cover your move as you go across."

"Are the Kashmiri boys ready?"

"Yes, Sir."

"They will move ahead of my men. If we are detected

by the Indians, they will draw their fire and give us advance warning. Call them here."

A group of three scared looking local boys came, escorted by one of the men from Aurangzeb's group. They were Kashmiri peasants, bewildered and unsure. Aurangzeb greeted them with forced cheerfulness, "*Ha bahaduron. Jihad ke liye taiyar ho?"* (So, are you ready for jihad?)

The men nodded uncertainly. It was obvious they had been coerced into joining the group.

"Good. Say your prayers. Remember, if you die you will go straight to heaven. You will lead the way. We will be behind you. We will leave at midnight. It will be the darkest then and will give us time to get across before dawn."

The group waited. The Pakistani bombardment intensified. Then, at a signal, they crawled up to the border fence and slipped through a small gap made earlier in the double fencing, "This will take you to the other side. You are on your own after that. Good luck."

One by one, the men crawled through the narrow gap and entered a grove on the other side. They spread out and reassembled. The scout gestured and the Kashmiri boys were pushed to the front to lead the way while the rest of the group followed, always keeping under cover.

They made their way through the wooded hills, going through gaps between the Indian posts. An Indian patrol passed by, coming to within 50 yards of where they were. Luckily, they had seen it in time and hid themselves waiting for it to pass. At that close distance, they could even hear the Indian JCO saying, "The Pakis are firing a lot today. They must be planning something. Stay alert".

After what seemed an age, the patrol passed by and Aurangzeb and his men moved deeper into India. They were not detected and by around four in the morning, reached the outskirts of Sopore, where they made their way to the safe house of a sympathizer. It had all been arranged beforehand. Aurangzeb signalled a halt short of the house, motioned his men to get under cover and then pulled out his satellite phone to make a call. The call was received by an elderly man inside the house – Dr. Mirwaiz. He was dressed in a night gown, but was awake and had obviously been expecting the call.

He did not say anything into the handset, but walked out of the door, and stood on the darkened road in front. He lit a cigarette, and Aurangzeb walked over to him, "*Islamabad se Srinagar kitna door hai?*" (How far is Islamabad from Srinagar?)

Dr. Mirwaiz replied, "*Bas, ab bahut nazdeek hai.*" (Quite near now). He walked back into the house and opened a door at the back through which Aurangzeb and his men entered in ones and twos. The men were pushed through a trapdoor into a cellar, leaving only Aurangzeb above ground. Mirwaiz covered the trapdoor with a rug, placed a table on top of it, and then turned towards Aurangzeb who hugged him reverentially, "*Bahut time hua hain. Hum aap ka bechaini se intezaar kar rahe the.*"(It has been quite a time. I have been waiting impatiently for you.)

The two of them shared a long association, and Dr. Mirwaiz had helped him a lot in his earlier missions in Kashmir. "How are things here now?"

Mirwaiz replied, "It is not as it was when you were last here."

Aurangzeb slapped him on his back, " *Wapis aa gaya hoon. Aur ab Aurangzeb ka sultanate phir yahan lagaoonga.*(I am back now and my reign will begin again). His voice took on a tone of hidden menace, "Remember, you are the only person who knows about me. It must stay that way".

"That is how it has always been, Aurangzeb *Bhai*."

"Good." Aurangzeb removed his cap and started peeling off the long scarf from around his face, "And Doctor *Saab,* there is one more thing you have to do for me before I start my mission."

Amar and Aurangzeb Prepare

Amar walked through his camp on the outskirts of the town. The camp was on a slight hillock and from there he could see the township in the distance, and the main road that passed through it after crossing the front gate of his camp, and disappearing in the hills beyond. In the early morning light, he could see activity around the shops and *dhabas* dotting both sides of the road, as they prepared for a new day. He always liked this time of day, especially if he wasn't out on an operation. It gave him time to pause and reflect, and perhaps soak in the abundant beauty of Kashmir. This was the only time he could see the hills and forests for what they were and not as likely ambush sites.

He went to a makeshift rifle range at the back of his camp, and slowly placed the Dragunov sniper's rifle he always carried, on a tarpaulin on the ground. His buddy, Sameer, set up a target exactly 100 yards away. Amar lay on the tarpaulin, picked up his rifle, fitted the scope and readied himself to zero in on it.

He aimed at the heart marked on the target, and muttered, "Take a deep breath; don't move; hear your heartbeat and fire between two beats, squeeze the trigger gently as you would squeeze a lemon...." He paused, keeping the heart of the target in his crosshairs and fired. A bullet hole appeared slightly left and below the heart.

He took a calliper from his pocket and adjusted the sights, muttering, "5 left, 3 down." The sights clicked as he adjusted them, and then took aim and fired again. A bullet hole appeared a little to the right and above the heart. "2 right, 1 down." He adjusted the sights again. Then very slowly and deliberately he fired again. This time the bullet hit exactly where he had aimed at – the centre of the heart – and he looked up satisfied. He took aim and fired three shots in quick succession. The bullets formed three small holes in the heart of the target, each hole virtually touching the other.

He kissed his rifle, "Perfect" and stood up with a smile. Behind him, his JCO, Subedar Ranjit Singh, who was watching with two others, clapped and called out, *"Badhiya Saab, par aap ke nishana kabhi nahin chukta hai."* (Very nice, Sir, you never miss)

Amar smiled back, self-consciously pleased at the praise, "I don't miss because I zero my rifle perfectly. All of you ought to do it too." He accepted a cup of tea which a soldier gave him, and walked around with it, easily mingling with his men. He joined them at the volleyball court, took the ball and served. It was a hard and fast serve, but the ball went straight into the net. His men laughed, "*Saab,* this time you missed."

"Pass the ball back, and watch this serve." He served again, this time the ball going wide and out. The men laughed and he laughed back. They shared that easy rapport that comes from months of living rigorously and sharing the same dangers, day in and day out.

One of his men came up to him, *"Sena Medal mubarak ho, Saab. Par app ko kam se kam Shaurya Chakra milna tha".* (Congratulations Sir, for you Sena

Medal but you should have got at least a Shaurya Chakra for your act.)

Amar looked a little self-conscious and fingered the line of ribbons on his camouflage jacket, a new red-and-white Sena Medal ribbon, on the top, "These things don't matter. The important thing is that we are safe and got rid of Ghazi and his *tanzeem*."

He turned to his JCO, "I have to go to the Battalion Headquarters. I may be late. Stay alert and don't let our men let their guard down. We can't take any chances here."

He got into the co-driver's seat of his Gypsy and driver Bajrang drove him away, a Quick Reaction Team (QRT) protection vehicle leading. He passed through the town, waving and calling out to the locals who waved cheerfully back at him. In the year or so he had been there, he had won the confidence of the locals with his fair and just manner. And the fact that he had managed to eliminate most of the dreaded terrorists who earlier operated with impunity, meant that security was returning to the area and small businesses could prosper. He passed a tea and provision store where Abdullah stood on the pavement, a cup of *kahwa* and a brass kettle in his hands. He waved him down.

"Not now, Abdullah, I have to be going, and am already late."

Abdullah insisted, "*Ek chotta cup, Saab*. I have made it just the way you like."

Amar accepted, and sipped the tea, still seated in his vehicle as he chatted with Abdullah. Abdullah was a steadfast supporter and often passed titbits of juicy information. Amar knew just how important in was to maintain good relations with the locals. He finished the tea, waved and drove on to the Battalion Headquarters, thirty kilometres ahead.

Commanding Officer Colonel Gurpal Sangha greeted him warmly, "Hello Amar. Congrats on your Sena Medal. You really deserved it."

"Thank you, Sir. It was your recommendation that got me this," He stroked the ribbon self-consciously.

Colonel Sangha was a tall, burly no-nonsense officer who was much loved and respected. And much feared for his temper in which he could unleash the choicest Punjabi abuses on anyone unfortunate enough to earn his ire. But like most Commanding Officers, he loved and cared for each member of his unit, and went to great lengths to ensure that they remained safe and as comfortable as possible.

"Your area has been quiet for a while now. The signs are encouraging." He continued, "But the battle against terrorism is not over when the last terrorist is killed. It is won in the hearts and minds of the people. We have to reach out to them even more. I want to conduct a program in your area, and I have an idea."

Amar nodded. A boss's ideas are not always good news. It would mean that he would have to implement them. "What, Sir?"

Sangha continued, "Have you heard of Maqbool Sherwani?"

"Of course, Sir. He was the local Kashmiri hero who diverted the Pakistani *qabalis* away from Srinagar when they raided Kashmir in 1947. He delayed them by almost 24 hours. He was crucified and tortured and brutally killed by the raiders, but his actions gained precious time which eventually saved Srinagar."

"He was from this area. He is a symbol of Kashmiri resistance and is quite revered here. On the request of the locals we have made an auditorium which we will name after him. I will get Umar Husseini to inaugurate it. He is the leader of the Kashmir Progressive Party and it falls in his constituency. He will be glad to do it."

Sangha continued, "I am planning to do this next month. And since it falls in your jurisdiction, ensure that the area is secure and the event goes off well." He paused, "By the way, we have been receiving intelligence reports of a new *tanzeem* coming up in your area. Apparently, it is headed by a Pakistani major from the ISI, a veteran who has been in Afghanistan and Kashmir."

Amar: "There has been no sign of any terrorist activity for a while now, Sir, ever since we eliminated Ghazi. Even my informers have not mentioned anything like that."

"Perhaps they are just waiting for the right moment. But keep your guard up, and intensify your patrolling. And during the inauguration of the auditorium ensure maximum security. There will be a large crowd there, and we can't take chances. Even a small incident could ruin everything."

Amar nodded reflectively, "I will do it, Sir." He saluted, got into his vehicle and drove back.

II

Aurangzeb was with his *tanzeem* in the forest. He had set up his group with care, using the core of the men he had brought from across the LOC. They had been joined by others and he now had around 15 good men – some who had operated with him in Kashmir and Afghanistan as well. He set up camp deep in the forest, but rarely remained with them. He came and left at will, sometimes disappearing for days at end, reappearing unexpectedly, staying for hours or days and then disappearing again. And during each of his appearances, he instilled an aura of fear within the group – something that was essential if they were to do his bidding to the death.

He had been with his group for a few days now, and was satisfied. He and his *tanzeem* were ready to act. He lay on the ground, covered with his traditional *keffiyeh* and *Mast Gul* cap, his *Badr* cradled in his hand. His eyes narrowed as he took aim at a pumpkin about 500 yards away. It had the face of an Indian soldier crudely painted on it – just two eyes and a mouth with an Indian helmet placed on top of it. His trusted aides, the brothers Majid and Sajid, knelt next to him.

Aurangzeb viewed the pumpkin through his sniper scope, zoomed the sights and brought it into clear focus. Then he placed the aiming mark between the eyes and gently squeezed the trigger.

The bullet hit the cheek and passed through. Aurangzeb, adjusted his sights and fired again. This time the bullet went cleanly through the eye. He adjusted the sights once again, and then reached into his pocket and pulled out a round of his special ammunition. It contained a gram or so of explosives in the bullet head, designed to explode on impact, and ensured that the victim would die of internal injuries even if the round had not hit a vital organ. He loaded the round in the chamber and fired. The round hit the centre of the forehead and the pumpkin exploded, the helmet hurled away and sent clattering to the ground.

He looked up at Majid with an evil smile. “We are ready now. It is time to let them know that Aurangzeb has arrived.”

The Inauguration of the Maqbool Sherwani Auditorium

Shazia adjusted her hijab and took a final look at herself in the mirror. The mirror was old and clouded, like everything else in the house, and her reflected image seemed a little hazy. But even that could not hide the pale translucence of her skin, the angular beauty of her features or the luminescence of her brown eyes. She had applied a little *kohl* around the eyes. She had selected her best *firhan* and shawl – though they were frayed and showed signs of age and neglect – just like the house itself. She was ready to leave now for the afternoon function and, in a way, she was glad for it. It would be the first time in weeks that she was going out of the house.

She took one last look around her room – the narrow wooden bed, a dusty bed sheet across it, the small window, which offered her the only view of the outer world, and the photos on the mantelpiece. There were just four with Asif in every one of them. Asif, beloved Asif, her younger brother, whose loss stabbed like a dagger in her heart each time she thought of him.

She picked up one of the photos and wiped it reverentially with the edge of her shawl. It showed the four of them, She, Asif, and their parents at a picnic they had gone to at Pahalgam. She was on a pony with Asif leading them and her parents following behind, smiling.

She remembered that day. A bunch of unruly tourists had passed some lewd comment about her and Asif confronted them like a tiger, forcing them to back off and apologize. That was Asif. He was only two years older than her yet he had looked after all of them with a maturity way beyond his years. When he left, he took all the smiles and happiness of the house with him. The house had become an empty shell after that; so had all of them.

She went down the steps from her room on the upper story of the house. Each step creaked as she did. Downstairs, she saw her parents sitting at their usual spot – the only corner of the house that caught the sunlight. Her mother smiled and rose as she approached, but the smile could not hide the sorrow in her eyes. After all, the sorrow had been a constant feature of the house – of her father, mother and she – ever since Asif died. Two years ago, wasn't it? Even now she woke up at nights with a muffled scream, dreaming of his brutal death; every day, she heard the prayers of her parents as they tried desperately to hide their sorrow. That house broke the day Asif died, and nothing would ever set it right again.

'I am going for the inauguration of the new auditorium, *Ammajan*," she called out. "Most of us from the school will be there. I will be back soon."

"Don't stay too long, and return before it gets dark, Shazia." Her father called out. He walked with her down the hillock that led to the track leading to the town and escorted her till the edge of the town before turning back. She pressed on, passed the school where she taught, and reached the open area where the Maqbool Sherwani Auditorium was to be inaugurated. The area had been under the shadow of terrorism for years, and it was a long time that an event such as this was taking place. She was looking forward to it. She would meet some of her students and the other teachers there.

II

At a large open courtyard in the township of Sopore, a large crowd of people had gathered. In the centre stood a bust on a tall pillar covered with a green cloth. Just behind the bust, was a new building, with the words 'Maqbool Sherwani Auditorium' emblazoned prominently on a board across it. A surprisingly large audience had turned up. In fact, it had been a while since such a large gathering had congregated at any one spot. Most of the town gentry was there, the prominent ones on chairs placed on the makeshift stage. The presence of Kashmir police and Army personnel, and the intensive security all around made the atmosphere relaxed and almost festive.

Captain Amar Rathore was also there with his men. He had been entrusted with ensuring that the event went off well, and was responsible for its security. His men were patrolling the hills overlooking the area and the streets of the town, but he knew how vulnerable security could be, especially in such a large gathering. But he had gone over each aspect in detail and was pretty confident, that he had it under control.

SP Altaf was there as well, along with his pretty wife, their four-year daughter gurgling happily in her arms. Altaf and Amar hugged warmly. Altaf laughingly invited Amar to dinner, saying he must be tired of the same camp food every day and "no one makes better mutton korma that my wife, Shagufta." Amar promised to go next week. It was a promise he would never be able to keep.

A roar of applause greeted Umar Husseini as he walked up to the stage and behind the rostrum. He was the sitting candidate of the Kashmir Progressive Party, one of the moderate voices in Kashmir politics, He raised his hands and began speaking in the tones of forced animation of a seasoned politician.

"We are here to honour our ancestor and hero, Maqbool Sherwani. As we all know, he was the man who saved Baramulla and Srinagar from Pakistani *qabalis* in 1947, though at a tremendous cost to himself. We are grateful for the hall that has been built in his name. It will be a place where we can meet and greet each other. We, too, have been through a period of great turmoil. We too have suffered at the hands of terrorists. But we have helped keep them at bay. And now we are ready for a period of peace and prosperity. We from the KPP will help make it happen...."

He droned on – a politician's speech – and as he ended to another round of applause, he turned to the audience for questions. Shazia raised her hand, and when Umar pointed to her, she spoke softly, "Sir, for peace and prosperity, we first need education. Everything else will follow."

Umar nodded in agreement, "Yes, I agree, but who are you?"

"Sir, I am Shazia Junaid. I teach in the local school here. Or rather used to teach. The school has not been functioning for months. The building, chairs, tables, blackboards and computers are broken down. Even the staff has not been paid and the children have stopped coming."

Umar nodded contemplatively. Like a seasoned

politician, he sensed an opportunity to make an impact, "I agree, there is nothing more important than education. From my party funds, I hereby release five lakh for the school. I will also speak to the authorities to ensure that the salaries of teachers and other staff are cleared at the earliest. Don't worry. We will have a fully functional school soon."

Even before he could complete, another voice rang out from the back, "All this is crap, *bakwas*. Don't give us all this talk of peace and development and education. What we need is justice."

A young man, wearing loose shirt and trousers, the ubiquitous *firhan* over them, walked up towards the rostrum. He held a white and red cane in one hand which he tapped ahead of him as he walked. He would have been handsome, but his face was pockmarked by scars, and his eyes were heavily bandaged with dark glasses over them. Security forces rushed to stop him but Umar waved them away and motioned him to come forward.

The man shouted out again, "Before you talk of peace and prosperity, talk about justice. Will you give me justice? For this?" He ripped open his *firhan* and shirt and revealed a chest pockmarked with pellet scars. "And for this?" He removed his dark glasses, and then began peeling off the bandage over his eyes. He threw the bandages and stared towards the stage, revealing scarred and mutilated eyelids and sightless eyes. He hit his cane hard against the floor, "Yes! Will you give me justice for this?"

The sight of the mutilated eyes forced many to flinch. The man stood there, arms akimbo, his body quivering from anger and tears running from his mutilated eyes. "TELL ME!!" he shouted again. As he did so, an old man ran up to him, put his arms around him, helped adjust his shirt and put back his bandages and glasses. He held him gently, as the man stood still trembling in anger.

The old man was Abdullah – the owner of the tea and provisions shop. He folded his hands and turned to Umar. "*Janaab,* forgive him. He is my nephew, Iqbal. He was hit by police pellets," he pointed to the scars on the chest and eyes, "and lost his eyes. He is angry and hurt."

Umar gestured, "I am sorry for what has happened. I promise all help will be provided to you. I will...."

The young man muttered, "Promises, promises. That is all we have been fed with all these years."

Some policemen came menacingly towards him, but Amar waved them off. He let Abdullah guide his blind nephew away, while Umar continued with his speech like a good politician. Amar realized that the tragedy of the young man was the tragedy of so many youths of Kashmir. Of so many young men who had been misled and then suffered tragically because of it.

Umar finished his speech and came down from the rostrum, unveiled the bust and cut the ribbon of the auditorium to a fresh round of applause. Then, like a good politician, he went around meeting people individually, had tea with them, chatted and listened to their problems. And then, as he walked back to his car, surrounded by his security men, a single shot rent the air.

The newly-unveiled bust of Maqbool Sherwani exploded, shattered by what seemed like a single shot. Whistles blew, and security personnel took positions, trying vainly to discern where the shot had come from. There was no trace. There was neither a wisp of smoke, nor a trace of where the shot had come from. It could have been from anywhere, from the hills overlooking the area, the roofs of the town, any place. But it was been fired so expertly that none of the security personnel who swarmed over the area had even noticed it.

Even as Umar was rapidly whisked away in his car, Amar looked around to see where the shot had originated. There was nothing. The only trace was that the shattered bust whose pieces lay strewn all over the ground. Amar picked up a chip. It was from the top of the forehead, but the groove of a bullet was clearly visible, directly between the eyes. The shot had been fired by an expert marksman.

Amar knew that the shot was more a warning, than anything else. He was right. On the very next day,, on the pillar where the bust had once stood, they found a placard with words crudely written in Urdu.

'THIS IS AURANGZEB'S FIRST SHOT'

Aurangzeb's Trap

Amar stood before Colonel Sangha, as the two went through photos of the shattered bust, and inauguration of the Maqbool Sherwani Auditorium. Sangha examined each one carefully, poring long and hard over those of the broken bust. He put down the photos.

"This is a clear challenge to us. Aurangzeb has announced his presence in our area. We should be prepared for more strikes. We were lucky there were no casualties this time. We may not be so lucky in the future."

Amar nodded. Sangha continued. "Intensify your patrolling and confidence-building measures. It has taken us years to get this area under control. It will take just a couple of strikes to lose all the gains of the past. And yes, activate your intelligence sources to get some information about him. From what I have seen about his modus operandi in the past, he hides incognito, surfaces to make a big strike and then goes into hiding again. Don't take chances."

Amar knew that Sangha was right. He increased his usual confidence-building patrols around the town but he could sense a shift in the mood. The townspeople were not as receptive and warm as before, and there was a faint tension in the air. As he drove through the town on one of his patrols, he passed the shop of Abdullah *Chacha*. His nephew, Iqbal – the same angry man at the inauguration

– was sitting outside, stick in hand. His face was a mask of anger and resentment.

He stopped to talk to them. Abdullah was one of the known 'friendlies', who was genuinely inclined favourably towards the Army. He had helped Amar gauge the mood of the town, and often made valuable suggestions from the local viewpoint which had helped tremendously. He stopped his vehicle outside the shop, deliberately left his weapon in it to show his trust, and went in.

"Ha, Abdullah *Chacha*, how are things? I notice your nephew is with you."

"*Janaab*, ever since I lost my own son ten years ago, this boy has been like a son to me. He lost his parents three years ago, and I have looked after him since then. He was studying to become an accountant when this ... happened."

"What happened to him?"

"The same thing that happens to so many of our children. He was studying in the university. Some of his friends told him to join a protest rally, and in the heat of the moment, he went there. The demonstration went out of hand, people began throwing stones, and the police fired pellets. My nephew was just standing with his friends, separate from the protesters, but was hit by the pellets and lost his eyes. I brought him here and got him treated. He has nobody else."

Amar knew what had happened to Iqbal was the tragedy of so many youths. He walked up to him. "Hello Iqbal, I am Captain Amar Rathore. I saw you at the inauguration. You seemed very angry. I can understand."

Iqbal turned towards the voice, and then turned away

saying, "You can never understand, *Saab*. So, spare me your sympathies."

"Listen, I know you are hurt, I know you are upset. But even Umar has promised to help get your eyes treated. I will help in my own way. I will find an eye hospital in Jammu or Delhi and, if need be, even pay for the treatment."

Iqbal snorted, "I don't want your help *Saab*. We can manage."

"Look Iqbal, I know you are depressed. Why don't you do something to occupy your mind? You are a trained accountant." He took out a note from his wallet, and put it in his hand. "You can differentiate our currency, can't you?"

Iqbal fingered the note, "Yes *Saab*. Your currency has a number written in Braille on it. It allows people like me to make out the note, after you have blinded us."

Amar ignored the jibe, "So, why don't you man the counter? You can maintain the accounts. It will be good for you and good for Abdul *Chacha* too."

Iqbal continued fingering the note and Amar realized that perhaps he had hit a chord. He continued his drive, passing the local school. It seemed to be functional now. Umar Husseini seemed to have kept his word. He could see Shazia, the same pretty teacher from the inauguration, taking a class outdoors. There was more activity than usual there.

He walked up to her. Even by the standards of the handsome Kashmiri race, she was very beautiful – and seemed intelligent and articulate too. "Hi, I saw you at the inauguration. I am glad your school is functional now."

Shazia adjusted her hijab, "Yes. Omar *Saab* had some funds released recently. Students and teachers have come back. We have resumed classes."

Amar tried to make conversation, when she adjusted her scarf and moved away. It would have been nice to talk to her some more, but Kashmiri women are notoriously reticent and conservative. It would not have gone off well. He turned back to his Gypsy and drove away, still thinking of her. His driver, Bajrang, watched him from the corner of his eye, with a faint smile on his face. He knew that the young Captain had been smitten.

II

SP Altaf finished his breakfast and looked at his watch. His four-year-old daughter was on his lap, slurping as he fed her breakfast, fascinated by his shiny buttons and cap. He was a little late, but it was okay. In any case, it was the only time of the day he had with his family.

He picked her up, threw her in the air as she squealed in delight and then gave her to his wife. He hugged her lightly, "Shagufta, I will be a little late today. But will be in time for dinner."

"You mean you will be here for dinner at midnight, as usual."

"No, no. I will make it back early today. But you don't wait up for me for dinner."

"You know, I always do. At least that way we get some time together. Go carefully now, *Khuda Hafiz*."

He got into the rear seat of his official car and drove away, an escort vehicle ahead and behind it. He drove through the town and as he did so, a *burqa*-clad woman whispered into her phone, "SP *Saab* has just passed."

Hidden half a kilometre away, Aurangzeb received the message, without reply. He fingered a *taweez* in his hands, kissed it reverentially, placed it on his gun barrel, "Guide my aim. Let my bullet strike my enemies." He cradled his gun. He was perfectly camouflaged and blended easily with the surroundings. Just the scope was visible, covered with a camouflage cloth to reduce the glint. He removed it, adjusted his sights, and zoomed in on the street in the distance. His sharp eyes squinted as he focused at the entrance of the police station, with its iron barricaded gate and the sand-bagged sentry posts. Altaf's car would slow down there, and he would have less than 10 seconds to execute the perfect shot.

SP Altaf's cavalcade of three vehicles zipped past. Aurangzeb took aim at the back seat where SP Altaf could be discerned behind the tinted glass windows and tracked the car till it reached the gate. Here it halted momentarily as the sentries shouted out, "*Jai Hind, Saab*," saluted, and opened the gate. Altaf, returned the salute, tapping his cane to the peak of his cap, as he called out, "*Jai Hind.*" Those were the last words he ever spoke. Even as he lifted his hand in salute, Aurangzeb fired, aiming marginally ahead to cater for the forward movement. The bullet shattered the window and hit Altaf cleanly on the side of his head, killing him instantly. His body was hurled sideways. His driver sped inside the open gate, the sentries took position, amidst blowing of whistles. But nothing followed the shot. Nothing could be seen. There was no flash; not even a wisp of smoke.

Aurangzeb watched the confusion below. He was too far to be detected. He kissed his *taweez* again, then took a serrated knife and carved a notch on the barrel of his rifle, "This is for SP Altaf." Then he picked up the empty shell and turned his rifle around towards the army camp in the distance, from where two vehicles raced out.

III

Amar was in his camp, when the phone rang. It was from the local police station and the sub-inspector on the line was completely distraught, *"Janaab. bahut bura hua hai. Altaf Saab, Altaf Saab...."*

"What! What happened to Altaf?"

"He was shot. Here. In our own police station."

Amar rushed out with his Quick Reaction Team, towards the police station just a few kilometres away. Altaf's body had been taken away, but his vehicle with its shattered rear window glass and bloodstained back seat still stood there. Scared police personnel manned the posts – looking for any sign of activity, or any hint of where the shot could have come from.

Amar's men formed a cordon around the area in a tight, well-disciplined movement. He rushed into the station, "What happened?"

The inspector blurted out. "Altaf Saab was shot, Sir. Right here." He pointed a finger towards his own head. "We don't even know where the shot came from or who did it. No one saw a thing."

Amar rushed out again. Less than twenty minutes had elapsed since the shooting, and perhaps the assassin was still in the area. He looked around from where the shot could have come. He scanned the area with his binoculars, along with his buddy, Samir, moving his gaze slowly across the warren of roofs of the township. His gaze fell on an overhead tank around 700 yards away. It was too far for an accurate shot, but it was the only position in the vicinity that provided a clear view of the police station.

Samir nudged him, "*Saab, woh dekhiye.*"

He gave him his binoculars and pointed to a corner of the overhead tank. There, on the second ledge, a cloth could be seen. It could be anything. But perhaps it could be something left behind by the assassin.

Amar focused closely on it. It seemed like the sleeve of an overcoat all right, with just its edge visible. The overhead tank was the only place from where the gunman could have shot Altaf. At that range, only an expert marksman could have made the shot.

He gestured to his team and they moved towards the overhead tank, reaching the base. A small piece of cloth could be seen, nothing else, no other sign of movement. An iron ladder rose upwards towards the ledge on the tank. He slung his rifle on his shoulder and told his men, "Cover me. I am going up to see."

His JCO, Ranjit Singh, came up to him, "*Saab*. I will go up. You give us cover like you always do. That way you will be able to see and hit the killer, if he is still around."

Amar realized he was right. He nodded in agreement. He looked around for a suitable vantage point from where he could cover the area He saw a two–storey building with a low roof. With swift, silent movements, he clambered atop it, with Samir by his side. He settled in a corner of the roof behind a water tank and looked at the maze of rooftops all around. The unseen sniper could be hiding in any of them. He focused on the overhead tank and scanned it carefully for any sign. There was nothing. It seemed clear. He motioned to Ranjit, and the JCO began climbing up the iron ladder to the top with another soldier behind him.

As they climbed slowly, Amar and Samir scanned the area covering the entire view in wide concentric moves. He focused again on the overhead tank. There was nothing to be seen.

Ranjit and his buddy climbed stealthily; their moves covered by Amar. The tension showed on their faces, which intensified with each step up. Ranjit reached the ledge and swung across. His buddy did the same. He gestured to his buddy to come from the opposite side. They cocked their weapons, and slowly moved advanced towards cloth.

They could see it more clearly as they came closer. It seemed to be an old overcoat. Ranjit indicated to his buddy to cover him as he approached it. He came up from behind and yanked the tattered coat off. Beneath it were two sandbags placed side by side. Next to them was a metal tube, crudely resembling a weapon barrel. Nothing else.

Ranjit looked down perplexed, and then realization hit him. He had walked into a trap. He turned too run, but it was too late. A bullet hit him squarely in the face, throwing him back, splattering his blood on the side of the tank. His buddy looked around confused, when the second shot hit him, hurled him across the railing, and sent him plummeting down to the ground.

There was no other sound.

Amar saw Ranjit and his buddy hit and fall. He looked around furiously with his scope, but could see nothing, no flash, not so much as a wisp of smoke. Around half a mile away, hidden on a distant rooftop, Aurangzeb smiled, his eyes narrowing wickedly as he did. He still twirled the *taweez* in his hand, as he caressed his rifle lovingly, "Two more to your name, *Badr.*"

He could see the confusion in the Army team as they looked around for a clue about where the shots had come from. They had not seen him, nor did they have any idea of his presence. He eased away from his hiding place, edged out of sight and disappeared into anonymity.

IV

Amar stood at attention while his Commanding Officer bawled him out. Colonel Sangha was in a foul mood and with reason, "Amar, what the hell is going on? In one day, we lost SP Altaf – one of the best police officers we ever had – and then two of your boys. What happened?"

Amar listened in silence as he waited for the tirade to subside. Then he replied, "Sir, Aftab was killed by a single shot fired at long range. It was not an ordinary gunman who did this. It was Aurangzeb. He also set up a trap for us, by luring us towards the water tank." He looked rueful, "and fool that I was, I fell for the trap."

Sangha calmed down, seeing the sorrow on his young officer's face. "Amar. The trap was for you. He hoped you would climb up so that he could kill you as well. He would have eliminated both the Army and Police chiefs of the area in one day. He wanted to make a statement."

He picked up a squashed bullet inside a plastic bag. "This is the bullet that was recovered from Aftab's body. It is a 7.92 calibre, larger and heavier than usual for greater stability at long range." He took out the bullet with a forceps and showed the bullet head, "And the bullet is tipped with an explosive charge, designed to explode on impact that will kill even if the shot does not hit a vital organ. Aurangzeb has been known to use this before."

Amar examined the bullet, "But I am quite a crack shot myself, Sir. I won the Army Rifle Association competition last year."

Sangha looked up "Amar, I don't doubt your capabilities. But this man is a veteran of many years. He has over 70 known kills."

Amar continued, "And I am pretty good at long ranges too...,"

"Amar, don't make this a personal duel between you and Aurangzeb. We have a bigger job to do. You focus on keeping your area incident free. We have the Assembly elections coming up. We have to ensure that they are held freely and without fear."

"That is my responsibility Sir. And don't worry. I got Ghazi. I will get Aurangzeb too."

Sangha looked worried as Amar saluted and walked out. He did not doubt Amar's capabilities. He was one of his best officers. But he was worried that emotions would get the better of him and lead him to make a mistake. He knew all too well, that one mistake could well be the last.

Amar attended Altaf's funeral the next day in which the dedicated police officer was laid to rest with full state honours. In his years in operations, Amar had seen many deaths, but this one shook him deeply. Altaf was more than a comrade; he was a friend who had welcomed Amar into his family. He saw his wife, numb with shock, their young uncomprehending daughter in her arms, and remembered the promised evening they were to have at their place. As the bugler played the Last Post, and the guard of honour fired their rifles in the air in one final salute, he watched the body of Altaf being gently lowered into the grave. He joined the line of mourners as they filed past, and poured a handful of earth on the coffin. He made a final promise to his old friend, "I will get him, Altaf. I will get him and take the gun with which he shot you. I promise you that."

Assassination of Umar Husseini and the Burning School

Aurangzeb walked into his hideout deep in the forest. He had just returned from an outing alone – as he often did. No one questioned his long absences. He would appear and leave at will sometimes for days at a time. He would stay with the group for hours or days – depending on his whims – before disappearing and reappearing again. It was part of a plan to ensure that no one, even in his immediate group, knew where he was or what he was up to. He appeared unexpectedly, a dead *hangur* deer slung over his shoulders. There was little blood on the carcass. It had been expertly shot with a single shot below the shoulders into the heart. He slung the deer down and two men came running to pick it up.

"Clean it and cook it well. We will have fresh meat for dinner." He sat on a rock and put down his rifle.

He started stripping his rifle, and cleaned each part meticulously. He picked up the barrel and peered through it. Majid asked, "*Janaab, mujhe de do. Main saaf kar leta hoon.*"

Aurangzeb laughed , "Your weapon should be like your *begum*. No one but you should touch her. Only then will she respond to you."

He finished cleaning his rifle, reassembled it and

cocked it a few times. He took aim at an imaginary target and pressed the trigger. He then smiled with satisfaction, stroked his rifle, and ran his fingers over the notches on the barrel, "See how well my *Badr* responds to me." He put it down reverentially, "But I am running low on my special ammunition. Get me through to Colonel Rashid."

One of his men ran up with a satellite phone. He erected the antennae swiftly and efficiently and stood it on a tripod on a rock, dialled and made contact with their handler in Pakistan; he handed the phone to Aurangzeb.

It was Colonel Rashid himself on the other side. He greeted Aurangzeb warmly, *"Salaam Aliekum Janab.* We have been receiving reports of your activities. It is in all the papers as well. Well done."

Aurangzeb laughed, "This is only the beginning. Watch what happens after this."

"The assembly elections are scheduled for next month. We have to ensure that they are not held. Create such an environment, that no one would dare to come out to vote."

"Don't worry. I will make sure that there will be nobody to vote for."

Colonel Rashid continued, "We have sent a fresh stack of currency and supplies, and your special ammunition. Collect it from the usual place."

"That is good. We were running low. *Khuda Hafiz.*"

He turned to Majid, "Organize the collection and make sure it is done in absolute secrecy." He picked up his rifle and disappeared into the forest where he had come from.

II

Around ten at night, two men closed in on to a house in the outskirts of the town. It was the house of Dr. Mirwaiz, large and affluent. Inside, Dr. Mirwaiz was sitting by the fireside, reading his newspaper, when his phone buzzed with a notification. It was a missed call from a number saved under no name. But he knew who it was, and what it meant.

He waited for a while, and then went around the house switching off all the lights, including the one on the porch. The area was in complete darkness. He then walked out wearing only his dressing gown, and lit a cigarette He leaned against a walnut tree smoking. He finished his smoke, tossed away the butt, and went back into the house.

The two men watching from a distance, waited for a while, and then slowly approached the tree he had leaned against. One of them scraped the ground beneath it, and removed the leaves and undergrowth. He dug a little, and groped around until his hands touched the top of a wooden crate. He scraped some more, widened the hole and pulled out the crate. They opened the top, just a bit. It was filled with tinned foodstuffs, wads of Indian currency, and cartons of ammunition.

They filled up the hole again. After covering it with dead leaves and twigs, they looked to see if there was anyone around, and then melted in the darkness.

III

The elections had picked up momentum in Kashmir, and the canvassing was reaching fever pitch. There were the usual calls by the separatists to boycott the election; some rabid political parties refused to participate, but overall, the approaching elections had generated considerable excitement. In the forefront were moderate groups like Umar Husseini's Kashmir Progressive Party.

Umar was campaigning extensively. This afternoon he was to address a rally in his constituency of Baramulla-Sopore. He decided to have it in the vicinity of the school – the same school that he had helped rejuvenate knowing that it would strike a chord with the locals. In an open ground adjoining the school, a stage was erected, adorned with flags of the Kashmir Progressive Party. The usual placards and hoardings with Umar Husseini's face were spread all around. A sizeable crowd had gathered and that in itself was an encouraging sign.

Umar arrived in his car, waving to his supporters as he did so. He was bang on time, a trait that had endeared him to his supporters. As expected, there was a large security presence of police and military personnel. Amar was there as well. After all, it fell in his area and he was responsible for the security.

Umar shook hands with the exaggerated movement of a seasoned politician, "Ah! Captain *Saab*. It is good to see you. After the unfortunate killing of Altaf *Saab*, there has been some tension in the area. Your presence will help give confidence."

Amar shook hands warmly, "Don't worry, Sir. We are here. But you do take great risks going around like this."

"Ah ha! As long as you all are here, I don't have to fear, do I?" He laughed airily and climbed up the steps to the stage. The audience cheered as he waved to them. Shazia was among them.

The entire scene was viewed through Aurangzeb's

sniper scope. He had concealed himself well as usual in a perfectly selected hiding place. The aiming mark followed Umar, rested long on Amar's head and scanned the audience where it lingered a little longer on Shazia. Then it moved back to Umar.

Umar was surrounded by his bodyguards and his face appeared fleetingly, weaving from side to side. He walked up to a rostrum at the middle of the stage, presenting a clear target to the sniper. The sniper scope was focused on his forehead as Umar began his speech.

"Bhaiyon aur bahenon. I am really happy to see such a large gathering of you here. It is a sign that things are changing. We of the Kashmir Progressive Party will help make the change come about. Vote for the KPP; do so freely and without fear, and together we will..."

Even as he uttered the first few lines of his well-rehearsed speech, he was thrown backwards and the banner behind was splattered with blood. He collapsed to the ground, even as security men formed a cordon around him. The crowd panicked, and the security personnel tried desperately to establish some kind of order. Whistles blew, and the Army established a cordon, trying to seal off the area. Amar himself raced around the perimeter, trying to see where the shot had come from.

On the stage, a doctor turned Umar's body over. His forehead had a single entry wound; the back of his head was shattered. They put him on a stretcher, placed him in an ambulance and rushed him away – but it was clear. It was already too late.

From his distant hiding place, Aurangzeb watched the scene through his sniper scope. He picked up his mobile, *"Rakh diya?"*

A *burqa*-clad figure in the audience whispered into a phone, "*Haan Janaab.*"

Aurangzeb moved his sniper scope to the school building adjoining the rally site. He focused on a pile of rags over a plastic can at one side. He aimed at the can and fired two rounds in quick succession. The bullets hit the can, petrol spurted out and slowly ignited. The fire spread rapidly, crawled over the wooden side of the building and spread outwards.

In the chaos of the rally, someone shouted, "The school building is on fire."

Amar and some of his men ran towards the burning building. Shazia also ran towards her beloved school. She joined a line of men who futilely poured water and sand over the fast-spreading fire.

Amar splashed the flames frantically with buckets of water Against the backdrop of the burning school, his head bobbed up and down in the sniper scope of Aurangzeb's rifle. Aurangzeb tracked him waiting for the perfect shot.

As they tried to control the inferno, Shazia went too close to the flames. A burning ember set her *dupatta* aflame but she was oblivious to it. Amar saw the flame climb up her *dupatta* and jumped forward, yanked it off with one smooth movement and hurled it away.

That movement saved his life. Even as he dived towards her, Aurangzeb fired. The bullet zipped over his head and crashed into the burning building. No one was even aware of the shot. Even Amar did not realize that he had escaped death by inches.

The movement hurled Amar into Shazia. He held her protectively, "Are you okay."

She nodded, “Yes, are you?” She disengaged herself gently and walked away. She turned around and her eyes welled with tears as she saw her beloved school blazing away. From a distance, the sniper scope rested long and lingeringly on her face.

Shazia walked back to her home, crushed and defeated. Her parents were waiting anxiously for her, as they always did, each time she went out. They had only to take one look at her dishevelled features, her soot-grimed face and dirtied dress to know that something terrible had happened. They rushed her inside. She sat at the table, covered her face with her hands and sobbed. The horrors of the past rushed back into her memory. She lifted her tear-stained face and cried out, “They are returning. Those days are coming back again.”

IV

Amar went back wearily back to camp. He had barely removed his helmet when Colonel Sangha rushed into the camp, along with his protection vehicles. He was livid.

“Amar, what the hell is happening in your area. We lost Umar, the school building was burned down. And all while you were there. All the gains of the past year have been washed out. Don’t you have any leads as yet? What has happened to your informer network?”

Amar waited for the harangue to stop as Sangha went around the camp, and then drove off in anger. As Sangha’s vehicle disappeared in the distance, he sat down wearily and called for his senior JCO, “Where is Tejpal?”

“*Saab*. He has gone to Romeo sector with his team.”

“Send a message for him. Tell him I want him here immediately.”

A few days later, Amar was outside his camp, near the main gate. As always, there was a crowd of locals there, each with some grievance they wanted him to address. He met them one by one. It was an act he always followed. It helped develop rapport and goodwill. Sometimes it got him some very useful information as well.

One of the civilians came up with folded hands, *"Saab, ham porter hai. Naukri dhoond rahe hai. Hame aapke saath laga dijiye."* (Sir, we are porters. We are looking for work.)

Amar asked, "How many are you?"

"Four, Sir."

"I don't need any porters right now. But the GREF camp is looking for workers." He scribbled a brief note, "Go there. I will tell the Commandant that you are reliable and good workers. They will hire you."

Another civilian came up, "*Saab*, we send consignments of walnuts and dry fruits to Jammu every week. On the way, our trucks are stopped for checking, the boxes opened and some of our produce is damaged. Please stop your soldiers from doing this."

Amar thought for a while, 'Okay, we will check the packages before you load and seal them. In that way we won't have to open the packages en route. It will prevent damage."

Another civilian came up and placed a box of apples at Amar's feet. *"Janaab, yeh dekhiye."* He took one and handed it to him. "These are the best apples in Kashmir. From my orchard there."

The civilian took out one more apple. Blood red, but

with a piece bitten from it, *"Aur yeh dekhiye*. This is from my orchard, *Janaab*. The best apples in Kashmir. But see. One of your jawans broke it and was eating it when I saw him. He threw the apple and ran. Here it is, *Janaab."* He gave the half-eaten apple to Amar.

It was late and Amar was getting irritated. "So, what is it that you want?"

"I want justice, *Janaab*. Compensation. Compensation for the damage caused to the best apples in Kashmir."

Amar whacked the man hard on the back of his head. "You want compensation, I will give you compensation." Then he smiled, "Come on in, Tejpal."

V

Amar sat with Tejpal in front of his tent, both men sipping tea from enamel mugs, a plate of *shakarparas* on a block of wood between them. There was an easy camaraderie between the two. They had been through a lot together and Tejpal was one of his most reliable informers. He was the one they called Joker, and it was his information that had helped him get Ghazi. But then Tejpal changed his appearances and name often. That had helped him stay alive so far.

Amar: "Just when things were coming back to normal after we eliminated Ghazi, this new *tanzeem* has come up. We know nothing about it, except that it is led by a Major Aurangzeb, who is a crack shot." He nodded with reluctant admiration, "That guy is good. He fires at long ranges, hits and disappears. He never misses."

Tejpal: "What about the local informers? Haven't they brought any information about this new *tanzeem*?"

"Nothing. None of the locals even speak about it. Either they don't know, or are too scared to say anything. Especially after SP Altaf was killed. That's why I called you here. I want you to locate this Major Aurangzeb and his *tanzeem* for me."

"Leave it to me, *Janaab*. I will find out."

"But how will you do it?"

Tejpal looked reflective, "I have been working in an apple orchard for too long. I think I will become a porter in the bus stand for a while. Or maybe a waiter in a tea stall. I will be able to find some information. People talk over *kahwa*."

Amar thought over what he had said. "Tejpal, be careful. You have been moving all over Kashmir in different disguises to get information. But it is dangerous. If the militants discover you, death is sure to follow. Why do you do take such risks?"

"Sir, my family is from Kulgam. My earliest memory as a six-year-old was of fleeing the village, because militants threatened all the Kashmiri Pandits there. I still remember those announcements on the loudspeakers and armed men pounding at our door, telling us to leave in 48 hours, or we would have to leave my mother and sisters behind. My parents have died, but I want to go back to my Kulgam, to the old Kashmir I knew. That is why I take these risks. So that we could go back some day."

Amar clapped him on the shoulder, "Good luck, Tejpal. Just be careful."

"*Fikr* not, Saab. I will find out about this Aurangzeb and his *tanzeem*."

The Attack on the Camp

Tejpal spent the next few weeks mingling around the locals. He became a porter at the bus stand, and sipped tea with the other porters in their shed, gossiping on the happenings. He was a local and it was easy for him to blend with them and his jovial easy-going style usually enabled people to open up to him.

After a while, he took up a job as a waiter in a tea stall, picking up information from customers and passers-by. In his new disguise, he was unrecognizable. And then, he came back to the camp.

Amar and Tejpal sat outside the tent, a small fire between them. Tejpal held a plate in his hands and wolfed down the food ravenously. Amar watched him eat and waited till he had his fill.

Tejpal sipped some water, wiped his mouth with his sleeve, and smiled, "*Janaab,* I have found something." He put his plate down, "A new *tanzeem* has indeed come up in the area. It is led by a Pakistani called Aurangzeb. He crossed the LOC four months ago."

Amar: "Any idea who its members are?"

"They are Pakistani and Afghan militants. Most of them have fought in Afghanistan or had come to Kashmir before. There are no local militants with them. No one seems to know more than that."

"But they must be having some local contacts. Some sympathizer who helps them."

"There is one man who could be it, *Janaab*. Mirwaiz. Doctor Mirwaiz."

Amar's eyes hardened, "I know him. We have been suspecting him of harbouring terrorists for a long time now. But we haven't been able to nab him because of his political connections."

"He is a known sympathizer, Sir. An underground worker, I know. I had watched his house for some time and three nights ago, some unknown men came, collected some supplies and went. They were not locals. They have to be part of Aurangzeb's *tanzeem*. Mirwaiz could be the man who can lead us to Aurangzeb."

"But how?"

"I will have to get into their *tanzeem, Saab* and go directly to Aurangzeb. I have a plan. But for that you will have to make the most perfect shot of your life."

He told Amar his plan. Amar recoiled, "No. No way. We cannot do it. It is too dangerous."

Tejpal held Amar's hand reassuringly, "*Janaab*, it is the only way. Trust me. We have no alternative."

Amar did not say anything but nodded reluctantly. He was not fully convinced of Tejpal's plan, but knew that there could be no other way.

II

It was late at night in the Army camp. Sentries were at their posts, the perimeter patrol was making a final round and searchlights were scanning the area outside. Amar walked around the perimeter himself, weapon in hand. He stopped and talked to the sentries in their sand-bagged enclosures and looked at his watch.

He was waiting for something. And that time was approaching.

Suddenly a shot rang out, then another, then a series of short bursts. The sentry at the sandbagged enclosure fell face down with a loud cry. More bullets rang out, hitting the outer wall. Whistles blew as soldiers rushed to their positions and began firing back. Another soldier at the gate was hit and fell with a loud cry. The sound of the fire was heard by the locals outside, who looked quizzically at each other, "*Fauji camp mein kuch ho raha hai.*" (Something is happening in the Army camp)

Amar rushed to the perimeter, rifle in hand. He switched on the night sights on his sniper scope and scanned the area beyond. He could see blinks of rifle fire coming from outside, but was looking for something else. He continued scanning till he saw a figure crouched behind a low mound, who seemed to be controlling the operation. That figure rose, fired once, and got behind cover. He rose and fired again. And again, slipped behind cover.

Amar took careful aim at the figure, adjusting his aiming mark, "God, let this shot be true." The figure rose again, exposed itself for a longer while and Amar fired. His aim was true. The bullet found its mark and the figure fell to the ground with a loud cry.

But the man was not dead. Even as he fell, he stood up again and even had the presence of mind to pick up his rifle. He ran back, holding his injured shoulder with one hand, in visible pain. He was wounded, but not dead.

Amar looked at the retreating figure through his scope. He could have fired again, but did not. Instead, he put his rifle down.

He lifted his hand to signal and the firing stopped from the camp. The sentry who was shot stood up, brushing himself, as did the other 'killed' sentry. Amar looked at the retreating militants, his face taut with tension.

He called his JCO, "Send two ambulances along with the QRT towards the Advance Dressing Station. They can come back without going in. And spread the rumour in the town that two of our soldiers were killed in a terrorist attack and two others wounded."

He paused and looked in the darkness, "Now we can only wait to see what happens."

Tejpal Contacts Aurangzeb

A wounded man staggered towards Dr. Mirwaiz's house. He looked around furtively, and then pounded on the door. Mirwaiz heard the sound and looked around quizzically. He took a pistol from a drawer and went to a window from where he could see the street below.

He could see the figure at his door, weapon in hand, obviously scared and wounded, looking around furtively. There was blood on his *firhan.*

His wife asked, "Who is it?"

"Nobody. One of us. Don't get out of bed." He walked to the door, gun in hand, and called out softly, "Who is it?"

"*Janaab, bacha do. Mujhe bacha do.*" There was pain and desperation in the voice.

Mirwaiz paused for a while and then yanked open the door. The injured terrorist staggered in. He folded his hands, "*Doctor Saab. Mujhe chuppa do. Bharatiya kutte mere picche hai.*" (Doctor, please hide me. The Army is after me). He fell in a state of semi-consciousness. He had lost a lot of blood.

Mirwaiz and his wife took the injured terrorist to the secret room in the basement and placed him on a bed there. They had obviously done this before. He told his wife, "Clean up the blood near the door. I will look after him."

He cut the bloodied *firhan* with a pair of scissors, and took it off. Beneath was a jagged bullet wound on the shoulder. "How did this happen?"

"*Janaab*. We had attacked the *fauji* camp. Even killed a few of the dogs. But I got hit and barely managed to escape."

Mirwaiz gauged the wound expertly. He had treated many such people before, who had come to him with similar injuries. He injected a painkiller, cleaned and stitched up the wound and bandaged it.

"You have lost a lot of blood. But the wound is not serious. You are lucky the bullet has passed through the shoulder and did not hit a bone; else it would have been worse. You have done well. Rest now."

The terrorist fell asleep and Mirwaiz took his gun, then checked his *firhan* and removed the cheap mobile phone from it. From its pockets, he took out some packets of dried fruit, some cartridges and a dagger – standard tools of the trade. He then went to his room and made a call, using a separate mobile from his drawer for the purpose.

The call was received by a tall *burqa*-clad figure. Mirwaiz asked, "Begum, was the Army camp attacked tonight?"

The voice replied, "Yes *Janaab*. We could hear the firing for a long time. A few of the soldiers were hit. We saw ambulances rushing out from the camp after that."

Mirwaiz nodded and disconnected. He looked reflective. He checked around one last time for any traces of the presence of the wounded man, and then switched off the light and fell asleep.

A day or so later, the wounded man was lying on the bed eating porridge. He was clean and looking healthier than before. It was Tejpal. As Mirwaiz walked in, Tejpal put the bowl aside, reached for the doctor's hand, and kissed it gratefully, "*Janaab*, you have saved my life."

"Who are you and how did this happen?"

"*Janaab*, I am Attaullah from the Reasi *tanzeem*. The army dogs had forced us out of the area and I came here. I heard that Aurangzeb *Saab* and his *tanzeem* are doing so much here. I want to join him and do what I can to help."

Mirwaiz inspected the wound and applied a fresh dressing, "Nobody can meet Aurangzeb just like that. But I will arrange a meeting with his emissary."

Around a week or so later, Tejpal was in bed. He had recovered well, and was not so heavily bandaged, though his hand was still in a sling. He sat up with difficulty as Mirwaiz came in.

"So, feeling better now? Good." He examined him, "Your wound has healed well. You are fit to move. You will meet Aurangzeb's emissary tonight. Get your things together."

As Mirwaiz went out, Tejpal went into the washroom to pee. He switched on his watch – an old, cheap-looking piece and switched on a hidden switch beneath its face. That switch activated a GPS signal, which beamed his position to the receiver.

This message was received by Amar on his receiver in his camp. He had been waiting a long time for that signal from Tejpal, and this small beep filled him with relief. He knew where Tejpal was now – the signal indicated that he was in Mirwaiz's house. He called his JCO, Om Prakash – a seasoned veteran who had been with him in many operations.

"Om Prakash *Saab,* I want six hand-picked men. If we take more, we may draw attention. We will move on foot so that we are not detected easily. Be ready to move out in the next thirty minutes."

Amar put on his bullet proof jacket and *patka,* and made a final check of his weapons and radio. He and his men said a short prayer at the small shrine in the camp and then stealthily slipped out of the rear gate. It was essential that no one should see their movement. There were informers everywhere and secrecy was of essence.

Inside Mirwaiz's house, Tejpal too was getting ready to move out. Mirwaiz came in and blindfolded his eyes. He did not protest; he knew that this was the standard procedure. He was led by Mirwaiz to a hidden trapdoor in the basement and guided into a tunnel, "Follow it. It will take you to the forest. You will meet whom you are looking for there." The trapdoor closed behind him, and Tejpal was alone in the dark tunnel.

Tejpal removed his blindfold as he crawled through the tunnel. It was longer than he expected – over 400 yards – and seemed never ending. After what seemed like an eternity of crawling, he finally came to another trapdoor at the end. He pushed it open, and emerged in a deep grove in the forest, squinting as he tried to orient his eyes to the changing light.

Amar had been following the GPS signal that Tejpal's watch emitted. However, as Tejpal entered the tunnel, the signal was lost. The blinking stopped.

'Damn, I have lost his signal."

Om Prakash came up to him. "*Saab,* there is Mirwaiz's house. This is where he was last. He has to be someplace nearby." They continued moving desperately towards it.

Tejpal dragged himself out of the tunnel and looked around uncertainly. He emerged over ground and tried to see what was around him. Slowly, he homed on to the figure of a large *burqa*-clad woman, watching him. He squinted in that direction, *"Kaun?"*

"Here." The woman walked towards him.

"*Kaun?*" he called out again. The terror was building up. He realized that there was something wrong. Very wrong.

The woman called out softly, "So you want to meet Aurangzeb, no?"

Tejpal: "Yes, I am Atta. From Reasi. I want to meet Aurangzeb and join him."

The woman's voice seemed mocking as she replied, "Ah! So, you are Atta from the Reasi *tanzeem,* right. But weren't you also an apple seller here? And then a porter in the bus stand? And then a waiter in a tea stall there? I have seen you there."

Tejpal remained silent. He knew he had been detected. He peered feebly towards the large figure of the *burqa* clad woman and tried to see what was around. There seemed to be nothing.

"So, you want to meet Aurangzeb, right? Well, you will meet him. After all, a man's last wish is always granted. There. He is right behind you."

Tejpal turned around in alarm and as he did so, a hand

grabbed his face. A serrated knife ripped across his throat. Tejpal fell gasping for breath, holding his throat as blood gushed out. Even as Tejpal reached out with his hand in a desperate bid to break the stranglehold, his watch beeped, and the watch face glowed. It was Amar. He had finally made contact with Tejpal – but at a terribly wrong time. A powerful hand reached out, ripped the cheap looking watch from his wrist and smashed it with the handle of his knife. Tejpal lay twitching on the ground and Aurangzeb wiped the blood on the knife on his tunic, watching him bleed to death. Then he turned to the *burqa*-clad figure, "*Begum*, you have done well. Take the body away and show what the fate of informers to the people."

He disappeared into the forest. Tejpal's body stopped twitching and lay inert on the ground. The *burqa*-clad figure came up to it, watched life ebb out and then hoisted it on her shoulder and walked into the forest with it.

Amar Avenges Tejpal

Amar and his team remained hidden in the area around Mirwaiz's house, where Tejpal's last GPS signal had come from, till it went silent. Amar tried calling him, pressing down on his own switch, in the hope that it would activate Tejpal's phone. It was a grave error. Tejpal's beeping watch was seen by Aurangzeb, who smashed the phone, and then there was nothing. No other message came. Finally, in the early hours of the morning, Amar called off the search for fear of being discovered and they moved back to camp.

He stayed awake, glued to his mobile and receiver hoping for some news when Om Prakash burst in, "*Saab, Tejpal mil gaye.*"

"What! That is great. Where is he?"

Om Prakash lowered his eyes, "They found his body in the town square. It was badly mutilated."

Amar and his team rushed to the place. There, tied to a pole was the body of Tejpal, a placard around his neck saying, "This is the fate of informers." The locals stood silent and sullen, none coming close. The body had probably been hanging there all night but no one dared cut it down.

Two soldiers brought the body down and carried it away. It had been badly mutilated, its throat ripped, tongue and genitals torn out, eyes gouged. Amar watched it being taken away with sorrow. Tejpal was more than an informer; he was a loyal friend – a man who took a great risk and died because he had been unable to protect him.

They returned back to the camp and Amar rushed into his tent. He grabbed his rifle, put on his bulletproof vest and shouted out, "Get the QRT ready, we are moving out." He ran towards his Gypsy and got into the driver's seat.

Om Prakash ran after him, "*Saab,* where are you going."

"I am going to get Aurangzeb. He did it. We are going to the hills where he will be. GET THE BLOODY QRT READY." He was almost in tears with anger and sorrow.

Om Prakash gently switched off the ignition, "*Saab,* that is what he wants." He waited for Amar to regain his composure and continued, "What was done to Tejpal was more than a message to the town people. It was a message to you. He wanted you to head out in anger, perhaps to ambush you. He wants you to take a rash step. Don't fall into his trap."

Amar calmed down, still trembling with anger, "I am not going to let him get away with it."

"*Saab,* we have one lead. Tejpal was last in the house of Dr. Mirwaiz. Mirwaiz is obviously the contact man for Aurangzeb. He will contact him again."

Amar burst out again and tried to restart the vehicle, "Let's go get that bastard Mirwaiz. I will tear out his eyes and make him talk."

Om Prakash switched off the engine again, "It will be of no use, *Saab*. We have no proof against him. There will be no evidence, and we will have only given away our hand. We have to be patient. Let us just continue watching his house. Something will turn up there."

Amar slumped against the wheel, "It is my fault that Tejpal has died." He stood up and composed himself, "You are right. We can't act prematurely. We will continue to watch Mirwaiz's house. But I can't risk any other lives. I will do it myself."

II

For weeks thereafter, Amar and his buddy, Sameer, kept Dr. Mirwaiz's house under surveillance. They went there every night, took up positions in a wooded grove a little distance away, heavily camouflaged in sniper suits, and kept a watch on the house with night vision binoculars.

The fatigue showed on Amar, but he was like a man possessed. He would go there virtually every night, lie awake observing it, and then get back to camp by early morning. He was all set to move out again, late one evening, when Om Prakash came up to him, and offered him a cup of tea, "*Saab,* it has been weeks at a stretch that you have been going out. Let me go today. You need the rest."

Amar smiled wanly, "I can't take a chance with any other lives. I will go." He set out on foot with his buddy, Sameer, and reached the vantage point where they waited.

Mirwaiz's house was in darkness. Even the porch light was switched off that night. Amar and Sameer were on the lookout for any activity. "I will take first watch. You sleep. Then you watch for two hours."

Sameer smiled, "*Saab,* in any case you stay up all night. I will also stay up with you."

They watched through night vision binoculars and the exhaustion began creeping up on Amar. Sameer passed him a tetra pack of fruit juice which he sipped slowly. His lips were cracked and eyes swollen with exhaustion. He peered through his binos and scanned the area up and down.

Nothing.

Even as he watched, the images started blurring. His hand shook and loosened, and the binoculars slipped from his hand and fell on the crook of his elbow. Sameer looked at him, lying in exhaustion, took the binoculars from his hand and continued watching. The exhaustion was telling on him too, and he too was fighting sleep, when he suddenly saw the back door open. Mirwaiz came out dressed in a night gown. Sameer nudged Amar who came awake in an instant and was immediately alert. He too trained his binoculars in that direction and watched Mirwaiz go to a tree, lean against it and light a cigarette, cupping the flame. He took a puff or two, crushed the butt on the bark of the tree, and walked back.

"Why the hell did he come out for a smoke so late at night?"

Through the night vision binoculars, they saw two figures come into view, moving slowly through the grove. One walked up to the tree, while the other covered him. He stopped at the tree that Mirwaiz had leaned against for a smoke, bent down and scraped the covering of leaves and earth around it. Both men dug into the damp earth and finally pulled out a wooden box. They filled the hole, covered it back with leaves and earth and faded into the shadows. Amar continued scanning the scene and took a video of it with his mobile.

Sameer: "There. Let's get them."

Amar lifted his hand, "No. We will follow them. They will take us to Aurangzeb's camp. But we will have to do it alone. If there are too many of us, we will be discovered." He made a call to Om Prakash in his camp.

"Om Prakash *Saab*, I have made contact. I am following them. Get your men ready. I will keep sending you my position. You follow me, but keep a safe distance behind. Close in only when I tell you."

Amar and Sameer watched the two terrorists walk away with their box, and slowly followed them. They kept some distance from them as they went along a long and winding path through the forest. After two or three hours they reached a small stream. Here, they abruptly dropped the box and walked away in different directions.

Amar was confused. Sameer said "Sir, they are going away. Let's get them."

Amar was all set to rise when he realized what was happening, "Wait." He crouched again, and continued to watch the box hidden behind a tree. "Someone will come for the box." They lay motionless, keeping a sharp lookout.

Sure enough, around half an hour later, two men came to the stream, washed their faces, walked to the box, picked it in one quick movement and began walking away. Amar and Sameer followed them cautiously, keeping a safe distance behind.

Amar sent Om Prakash his live location on the GPS. "This is my location. Come here."

Om Prakash had been waiting for this message; his men were primed and ready, and they set out on foot to avoid being seen. They moved rapidly, following Amar's location. Ahead, Amar and Sameer continued following the two men, moving in the pitch-dark night more by instinct, than anything else. Every now and then, they switched on their night vision binoculars to check if the two they were following were still in sight. They went deeper in the forest, slowly climbing towards the upper reaches of the mountain. Gradually, the sun appeared as the first light of day broke through the wooded hills. There was enough light to see now.

The two men halted. One of them whistled softly; someone answered likewise from the forest.. A man walked out of a grove dressed in a bullet proof jacket and carrying an automatic rifle. He was followed by another. They had obviously been expecting the two men. They waved them towards a clearing that was so well camouflaged that it could hardly be noticed. They carried the wooden crate to where Majid and Sajid were sitting by a small fire and handed it over to them.

"At last! We were getting low on supplies and, more than that, on ammunition. Are you sure you were not followed?"

"Yes *Janaab*. Rafiq and Imran carried it to our usual place and we picked it up from there. Nobody followed us. We changed routes thrice to make sure."

Majid opened the box and examined the contents one by one. As he did so, Aurangzeb strode into the clearing. He had been away for days, but when he arrived, he entered unseen, and was virtually on top of them when the men became aware of his presence – as always. Even the sentries had not been able to detect his arrival. He moved like a ghost.

The men stood up reverentially. Majid bowed and pointed to the box half-opened on the ground, "*Janaab,* we have collected the supplies and your ammunition. There were a lot of currency notes also."

Aurangzeb looked into the crate and picked up two cartons of his special ammunition which he stuffed in the folds of his *firhan,* "Just in time. I was getting low."

He rifled through the contents of the box and looked up, "This will keep us going for a month." Suddenly, he sniffed the air, twitching his nose in different directions, almost like an animal sniffing the air for danger, "We will shift camp now. We cannot take a chance of these two been seen while coming here. Get ready to move."

The men started preparing to break camp. The fires were doused and covered with mud. The pup tents and sleeping bags were rolled up, and the weapons gathered. A man muttered to another, "This is the second time we are moving in three days. We had just come here."

Majid came up and whacked the man on his head, "Don't grumble, Aurangzeb *Saab* says don't take any chances. Do as he says!"

From a distance, almost half a kilometre away, Amar and Sameer saw the scene unfold. Even though they could not see what was happening, it was clear that the Aurangzeb was preparing to shift camp. Amar picked up his radio and hissed, "Om Prakash, where are you?"

"*Saab,* half an hour or so from you."

"Move faster, damn it. They will get away."

The JCO and his men had reached the base of the mountain and were moving upwards in slow deliberate movements. They were still too far. Amar knew that Aurangzeb's men would move out in twenty minutes or so – maybe earlier – and he had to slow them to enable his own men to come close.

He called out to Sameer, "Come with me," and the two crawled through a thicket that brought them within 400 yards or so of the camp. He could see the camp better from here, even though it was still indistinct. He tried to peer deeper hoping to locate Aurangzeb. But he had never seen Aurangzeb. He did not even know what he looked like.

He could see a person giving directions. He did not know it then, but it was not Aurangzeb, it was Majid urging the others to hurry up. They were all set to break camp. If they left now, all their efforts would be wasted. The terrorists would simply disappear and then it would be impossible to find them again.

Amar crawled even closer. He had to delay them somehow, and give time for Om Prakash and his men to reach there. Otherwise, it would be too late. He could see the silhouette of a sentry, and then another, some distance away. He took aim at the nearest sentry, and fired, dropping him instantly. The other one, alerted by the shot, dived and disappeared from view, as Amar's shot passed harmlessly over him.

But the sound of the shots had created the panic Amar had hoped for. No one could see where the firing had come from. A terrorist revealed himself fleetingly and Amar fired again. The shot found its mark and dropped him to the ground. Amar had fired three rounds so far without being detected from a perfectly camouflaged position, and his actions had forced the militants to take cover. He had managed to delay them, but hoped that Om Prakash and his men would reach there soon.

Aurangzeb did not see the shots fired by Amar, but immediately gauged the general direction they had come from. He trained his own rifle towards it, knowing that Amar would try to change his position and that movement would give him away.

However, Amar did not change position. He lay there perfectly still, not daring to breathe. From behind him, he heard the sounds he had been desperately waiting for. Om Prakash and his party had arrived and were closing in. One of the militants shouted out, "*Wahan se fauj aa rahi hai.*"

The approaching Indian soldiers could be seen as they charged up the hill, and Aurangzeb fired, hitting the leading points man. The rest of the soldiers went to ground, seeking cover. The fire fight between the soldiers and the militants intensified, and from his concealed position Amar fired again, killing another militant. By now, Om Prakash had managed to set up a light machine gun and a barrage of bullets swept the militant camp.

In the pitched fighting, the soldiers definitely had the advantage – both in numbers and in the quantum of fire they could deliver. Aurangzeb knew he had to get away. He shouted to the two men on his left, "You two give covering fire." He turned and with a bodyguard on either side sped towards a small bund, around four feet high. Beyond it, he would be safe. He vaulted across the bund and tried to get away from the camp around which the Indian soldiers were closing in.

But Amar had anticipated the move and his sights were focused on the exact spot where he expected Aurangzeb to appear. He was right. As the three militants jumped across the bund, he fired. The bullet hit the militant on the left of Aurangzeb, striking him in mid-air and hurled him sideways. He had taken the bullet meant for Aurangzeb, who jumped across to safety and disappeared in the forest.

Behind them, Om Prakash led a final charge on the camp. Amar and Sameer joined the charge as well, running in from another direction and firing from the hip. By the time they hit the camp, six or seven bodies lay on the ground, but the rest had fled – including Aurangzeb. He could see some of them disappearing in the distance. Amar weighed his options rapidly. He could chase the fleeing militants, but in those hills his men could be led into an ambush. He halted his men, and stood in the smouldering camp. As his men searched the area, in an adrenal-charged moment of exhilaration, Amar lifted his rifle and fired thrice in the air, shouting out triumphantly.

"Remember me, you bastard. I am Captain Amar Rathore. And I am going to get you."

Aurangzeb had crawled through the undergrowth to safety, along with a few of his men. But he heard the shout – as all of them did – and paused and looked behind. His eyes darkened with anger, "I will remember, Captain *Saab*. I never forget."

The Arrest of Mirwaiz

Amar and his team scoured the remnants of the camp looking for anything that might have been left behind. The found the bodies of the dead terrorists and examined them one by one. It was a huge success, and in spite of their own losses, the mood was one of elation.

Om Prakash came up to Amar, "Six. We got six of them. This is our biggest catch ever."

"Yes, but the prize catch got away. Aurangzeb. He is the one I wanted." He paused, "But I know how we can still get him. Come with me."

Bajrang had brought Amar's Gypsy as near as he could. Amar ran to it, got into the driver's seat and raced away, followed by his QRT and another vehicle containing the rest of his team. As he passed a fork in the road, Bajrang, asked, "*Saab,* where are we going? The camp is that way."

"We are not going to our camp. There is someone I want to see first."

They zipped away and reached the door of Mirwaiz's house. This time, there was no pretext or subtlety. The men established a cordon following time-tested drills, and Amar walked up to the door and kicked it open.

Mirwaiz was sitting on a sofa, reading a newspaper. His face remained expressionless, "Captain *Saab*, it is a pleasure to see you. But if you wanted to enter you could have rung the bell. Why break down the door? But then, the Indian Army has the habit of entering houses of innocent Kashmiris this way, no?"

"The army does not enter the houses of innocents, Doctor *Saab*. I believe a lot of people come and go into your house, especially at odd times."

"I am a doctor, Captain. A lot of people come to me and I treat them, irrespective of when they come."

"Including these people, doctor?" Amar pulled out his mobile and showed the video he had taken the night before of the two militants in the garden.

Mirwaiz looked impassive, "So, two people came here. What of it?"

"Search the house."

The men went around in a well drilled motion, searching the house room by room. A team began digging in the garden, next to the trees. Mirwaiz saw them and lost his composure. He came threateningly towards Amar and shouted,

"What! What right do you have to barge into our houses and damage our property? Why are you destroying my garden? Stop it immediately, Captain *Saab*. You don't know my connections. I will have this harassment printed in every paper in Kashmir. I will have you court-martialled and jailed. Stop it now or....."

He pulled out his phone to make a call when one of the men came running from the garden with a wooden box in his hands, "*Saab,* we found this buried in the garden."

Amar turned his gun towards Mirwaiz and pointed the barrel at him, "Don't move. Open the box."

Mirwaiz stood where he was. One of the soldiers ripped open the top of the wooden box to reveal wads of currency, tinned foods, first-aid kits and boxes of ammunition, even some grenades.

Amar picked up a tin. It had Pakistani army markings. He showed it to Mirwaiz without speaking. He picked up a box of ammunition, containing 10 large bullets – longer than usual. They were the special ammunition that Aurangzeb used.

"Where did this come from, Doctor *Saab*. It has Pakistani markings on it. And what is this ammunition? Who is it for?"

Mirwaiz sat down heavily on the sofa, "I know my rights. I want a lawyer."

"You will get a lawyer, all right. But in police custody. And there you will answer our questions." He waved the carton of ammunition, "Who is this for? Is it for Aurangzeb?"

Mirwaiz began protesting, and Amar called the police officer with him, "Take him to the police station." The officer pulled out a pair of handcuffs and walked towards Mirwaiz.

Mirwaiz suddenly stopped protesting. He seemed deflated and resigned to his fate, "Okay, Captain *Saab*. I will come with you. Can I take a few of my things with me?"

He called to his wife who was watching open-mouthed from above, "*Zara mere kapde le aana. Bus ek raat ke liye. Maen jaldi wapis aayonga.*"(Get me my clothes. Not much. Just for a night or so. I will be back soon)

He walked to a corner and reached out for something. Amar was instantly alerted, "What are you doing, stay away."

He picked up a cane from the stand. "My walking stick. Don't tell me you are scared of an old man's walking stick, Captain *Saab*."

"C'mon, let's go," Amar pointed towards the door brusquely.

Mirwaiz walked to a chest of drawers on the side, "I know you will be alarmed if I open it. But my medicines are inside. May I take them?" He opened the drawer very slowly and from inside pulled out a plastic medicine box, which he opened very deliberately and showed to Amar, "My diabetes and blood pressure pills. I need to have them every day. With your permission, can I take them with me?"

Amar nodded, and then in a swift movement Mirwaiz picked a capsule and put it in his mouth, "Aurangzeb will avenge me." He bit down hard on the capsule and fell to the ground, twitching. He was dead in less than five seconds. It was cyanide.

Amar rushed to revive him. His wife was screaming. But it was too late. Mirwaiz was dead, and with him, the only contact Amar had that could lead him to Aurangzeb had gone as well.

III

Aurangzeb took the remnants of his *tanzeem* to a new hideout, even deeper in the forest, and in the highest reaches of the mountains. It would be difficult staying there, but the place provided cover and protection from

Indian patrols. He watched his sullen and dispirited men set up camp, and waited till they had finished. He then called Wajid.

"How did the Army find our camp?"

"Wasim and Akram had just collected the supplies, *Janaab*. Maybe they followed them."

Aurangzeb walked up to two militants who were kneeling on the forest floor, cowering in fear. He slapped both of them hard across their faces. Again and again, repeatedly till their faces were bloodied and swollen. "How could you allow yourself to be followed?"

"*Janaab,* we took all the precautions you told us. We changed routes thrice. We don't know how the captain still managed to find us."

"Still managed to find you? Still managed to follow you? And you don't know how?" He mimicked them and continued slapping and punching them repeatedly, and then kicked them in the head and stomach as they fell pleading to the ground. Then, very deliberately, he pulled a pistol from his belt, and cocked it. He shot them one at a time, shooting them in their heads as they lay cowering on the ground. There was pin drop silence in the camp, as he stood over the bodies of the two dead militants. No one dared move. And then the tall *burqa*-clad figure appeared in the clearing. Like the others, she too was trembling in fear at his anger.

He glared at her, "What are you doing here, *Begum*? I told you not to come unless absolutely necessary."

'*Janaab*, some bad news. I had to tell you about it. The house of Dr. Mirwaiz was raided yesterday. The captain himself led the raid."

Aurangzeb turned round, instantly alerted, "What? Where is Doctor *Saab*?"

Begum paused and swallowed, "He is in *janat, Janaab*. He embraced *Shahadat*. He killed himself before they could extract any information from him."

Aurangzeb heard the news impassively and his eyes turned cold. He did not say anything for a long time, as he composed himself. Then he turned to Begum, "Watch every move of that fucking Captain. Where he goes, what he does, whether he is bloody masturbating in his bed, everything. I want every movement of his to be reported to me. Get me? Everything."

Begum shuffled away, and Aurangzeb spent the night with his men in their new camp. That night, as he lay in his sleeping bag, he could hear his men talk. They were speaking about the Captain.

"He got Salahuddin and Ahmed with one shot each. And it was so far, I could not even see the smoke."

"Yes, and he hit Akmal in mid air. *Yahan*." He pointed to his temple.

Aurangzeb heard the men talk and stood up. He walked towards the men, who became silent as he approached. He lifted his rifle and placed it on his shoulder. "I will find the Captain. And then I will show him what marksmanship is all about." He pointed his weapon at a chinar tree in the distance, aimed at a leaf, and fired. The bullet made a neat hole in the centre of the leaf. It was such a clean shot that the leaf did not even fall.

The Killing of Amar

Amar's successful raid on Aurangzeb's camp had got him a lot of kudos. In many ways, it made up for the reverses of the past few months. They had crippled his *tanzeem* and eliminated six of his men. But Aurangzeb was still on the loose. It would be just a matter of time before he struck again. He couldn't afford to let his guard down.

The news of the successful raid on the camp had percolated to the town – as these things often do. As the *burqa*-clad figure walked through the town amongst other women shoppers, she heard the gossip. One of them said, "I heard the army raided Aurangzeb's camp. We saw the bodies being brought to the police station."

"Maybe Aurangzeb himself has been killed."

"Aurangzeb is too smart for that. He will not get caught, and he will take revenge. He always does."

She walked down the main road, a wicker basket full of vegetables in her hand. In the distance she could see Amar's camp, with its barricades and sand-bagged sentry posts. There seemed to be heightened security there. The gates opened and a QRT vehicle emerged. Behind it, was a Gypsy with Amar in his usual camouflage jacket sitting in the co-driver's seat. The two vehicles crossed the outer gate and then zipped away.

She watched the vehicles go past and went to a secluded spot, where she took out her mobile and called an unmarked number. "Baramulla road. *Do gaadi.*"

The call was received by Aurangzeb. He listened intently and replied, "He will return the same way. Keep a watch of the road. I will come there myself." He wrapped his scarf even more tightly around his face, picked up his rifle and walked away rapidly.

II

Amar chatted easily with driver Bajrang, as they drove past the beautiful scenery on the way to Baramulla, where the Battalion Headquarters was located. His convoy entered the camp, and he walked to the Operations Room, where other officers were waiting as well, talking amongst themselves.

"Another conference. It will go on for hours as usual. Once the Old Man starts, he doesn't stop."

"Yes, but hopefully they will give us a good lunch. That is the only advantage of coming to Headquarters. The food is good, even if the conferences are boring."

The officers laughed and joked amongst themselves as they entered the conference room. Colonel Sangha was conducting the conference – the usual review-of-the-situation. He greeted his officers warmly and began, "Gentlemen, we are in a critical phase. As you know, winter is setting in. With snowfall, there will be a reduction in infiltration and terrorist activity. So, the militants could be planning a big strike or so, before the snows begin."

The officers nodded and took down notes. Sangha continued, "My aim is to keep our AOR incident free." He pointed towards Amar, "You have had a great success with your last raid. But intelligence reports say that Aurangzeb is still at large. He must be planning a strike in your area. I want you to intensify patrolling and be especially careful. And remember, I don't want you to get into a personal duel with him. Keep your area incident free, that's all."

III

Aurangzeb had moved rapidly to a location that gave him a good field of fire and observation along the road on which Amar was to return. Begum was in her hiding place, a little away. She would give him the advance warning required. He evaluated two or three different positions, before he finally homed in on a hollow in the ground, surrounded by shrubs. A fallen tree just ahead of it, gave him complete cover, and enabled him to fire without being seen. He camouflaged the sides of the hollow with small twigs and branches, and then covered himself with a large, leafy branch. There was nothing visible of him, or his rifle. Even his barrel and sights were covered by the folds of his large scarf, to prevent any glint or reflection. He slid into position, and waited.

On the opposite side of the road, a kilometre or so ahead, a *burqa*-clad figure moved into an abandoned brick kiln. She took position behind a pile of bricks, clearing out a small gap between them, so she could see the area ahead. Then she lay down, raised her binoculars to her eyes, and watched the road ahead.

The long day passed. The captain's vehicle was nowhere to be seen. Aurangzeb took a small sip of water, swirled it around his mouth and spat it out. He did not drink, since it would make him want to urinate, which could make him move. He remained still and silent, unmoving and patient.

Below, the *burqa*-clad figure looked at her watch. It was almost five. "I hope the Captain has not taken another route," she muttered to herself and then focused on the road.

In the distance she saw two vehicles approaching. She trained her binoculars on them, and could make out the Captain's Gypsy, following the protection vehicle, around fifty yards behind. Both the vehicles were moving fast. She spoke on her mobile, *"Aa raha hai."*

Aurangzeb focused even more closely on the bend in the road where the vehicles would emerge. He would have time for just one shot, but that was enough. The protection vehicle came into view, moving at high speed. He focused on the spot and his finger closed on the trigger, his left hand holding the barrel with the *taweez* clutched in it. As always, he spoke to his rifle, "One shot. One good shot, my *Badr*."

The Gypsy took the bend and entered into his sniper scope vision. It was moving very fast and he decided on a heart shot, rather than a head shot. He focused on Captain Amar, sitting in the co-driver's seat with his trademark jacket, and aimed at a spot just above the line of ribbons, near the newly received Sena Medal. At that speed, he had less than three seconds to aim and fire, but it was enough. His round shattered the windscreen on the co-driver's side and smashed through the jacket into the heart, killing instantly. The lifeless body was thrown back against the seat, and then bounced forward and slumped against the dashboard.

In the shock of the impact, the driver veered his vehicle off the road and careened into a ditch. The protection vehicle stopped as well, as the men took positions all around, trying to gauge from where the shot had come. Nothing was seen. Not a flash, not even a wisp of smoke. There was no trace where the shot had come from. Nothing.

From her hiding place, Begum radioed, "You got him. The Captain is dead. I can see him." She could see the Gypsy in the ditch by the side of the road, the Captain's body slumped across the dashboard.

Aurangzeb smiled. He then eased out of cover and moved back through a concealed route that he had reconnoitred earlier. The Begum too slipped out of her hiding place and disappeared into the forest. Night was just falling, and the darkness helped cover their movements. Aurangzeb moved back undetected, and when he reached his hiding place, he unslung his rifle, removed the serrated dagger from his belt and made a notch on the barrel of his rifle.

"This one is for the Captain."

After the Ambush

At the ambush site, the men gradually gathered themselves. Slowly the driver got up from the ditch where he had taken cover, and went cautiously to the co-driver's seat, his eyes still scanning the forested hills for any signs of activity. On the co-driver's side, the body lay slumped over the dashboard. Shards of glass from the shattered windscreen sprayed the back of the jacket, on which a dark red stain was slowly spreading. The stain covered most of the upper back, almost to the Captain's epaulets on the shoulders. His hand trembled as he reached out, paused for a while, and then as gently as he could, he pulled the body back, resting it against the seat. A blood stain covered the chest as well, moving across the line of ribbons – including the newly added Sena Medal. The chin and parts of the cheek were smeared with blood; the rest of the face seemed untouched, wearing a slightly bemused expression, the eyes partially open.

The lifeless face lolled to the side as the body shifted. But it was the face of the driver, Bajrang. Not Amar.

A FEW HOURS EARLIER

Amar had just walked out from the conference hall at the Battalion Headquarters. It had been a long conference as always and it was almost four. It could have gone on longer had it not been for the fact that all the officers had to be back in their camps before last light for security reasons. He shook hands all around, spent some time chatting with the Adjutant who filled him with the news of the rear and walked back to his vehicle. It was a long boring day and he was waiting to get back to his own camp. As he reached his Gypsy, he saw his driver, Bajrang, clad only in his combat dress and obviously feeling the effects of the early evening chill, though trying hard not to show it.

"Bajrang, what happened? You did not carry your jacket."

"No, Sir. It was not so cold in the morning. I did not think I would need it."

"Bajrang, you are a fool. You know how fast the weather changes here." He peeled of his camouflage jacket and handed it to him. "Here wear this. I have a jersey underneath."

"No Sir, I will manage."

"Don't be silly. Put it on." He got into the driver's seat, "I will drive. It will help wake me up after that boring conference."

They drove off with Amar in the driver's seat, and Bajrang in the co-driver's seat, wearing the Captain's jacket. He drove expertly, as he usually did, his thoughts lulled by the beauty of the area through which they were travelling. As it did ever so often, the stark disparity of the beauty and the violence that simmered beneath the surface hit him. He weaved his way across the wooded hills, his QRT vehicle leading the way, with its light machine gun mounted on the body scouring the area ahead. He kept a good 60 to 80 yards behind it, not too close, to avoid both could be targeted with one burst of fire, and not too apart, where they could be separated in case of an ambush. He had travelled this way ever since he had been posted to the Valley and, as it happens to even the best of soldiers, a slight sense of complacency had set in. His mind was drifting, and as he looked to his right at Bajrang, wearing his combat jacket, he noticed with a smile, that Bajrang seemed to be almost dozing off himself.

He nudged him lightly, "*Neend aa rahi hai?*" (Are you feeling sleepy?)

Bajrang jerked awake, "*Nahi Sahab,*" when the windscreen shattered and Bajrang's body was hurled backwards with the impact of a heavy calibre bullet striking him. The body hit the back of his seat, and then was hurled forward again, as it came to rest on the dashboard. The shock of the shattering windscreen and the impact caused Amar to swerve violently to the right, sending the vehicle off the road into a ditch adjoining it. Even as the crippled vehicle came to a halt, its rear wheels in the air and still spinning, he jumped out, carbine in hand and took position behind it. Ahead of him, his QRT team took up positions on the side of the road. The LMG unleashed bursts of fire at the wooded hills around them, but it was largely speculative random fire. Neither he, nor his team could see any signs of human presence around them.

He waited for another burst of fire to come towards him, as it usually would in case of an ambush. There was none. There was only pin drop silence, broken by the staccato of the LMG. He raised his hand in a signal for the LMG to stop firing.They were only wasting ammunition and merely giving away their exact location to the unseen attackers. He grabbed his binoculars and scanned the area. There was not a glimpse of movement or sign of any activity. He fired once or twice at what he thought would be likely hiding places, but there was no reply. The attacker had fired unseen – one single shot – and vanished.

It was Aurangzeb. It was his classical signature shot. Ahead, his QRT team moved ahead towards the hills, covered by their LMG, but he waved them back. It was pointless taking a chance and risking more casualties. And in any case, there was no one there. He called his men back, and he turned to the co-driver's seat, and pushed Bajrang's body erect. His jacket was soaked in blood. The bullet must have hit the heart, just above the line of ribbons he was so proud off. Bajrang was dead of, course. His eyes half-closed, his face a permanent mask of bemusement. For a moment, the thought hit Amar, that his last action was to mildly reprimand him for dozing, and cursed himself for giving him his jacket and letting him sit in the co-driver's seat while he took over the wheel.

Amar looked at the body, remorse on his face. "That bullet was for me. He took it. If only I had not given him my jacket."

His QRT commander came up, "You could not know it, *Saab*. Don't blame yourself for it."

Amar tried frantically to check for a pulse. He could detect none. He shouted out, "Let's take him to the Advanced Dressing Station (ADS). There may still be hope."

They righted the Gypsy from the ditch and raced towards Baramulla where the Brigade ADS was. Bajrang's body lolled in the co-driver's seat, as Amar held him by one hand, steering with the other, driving at breakneck speed, all the time saying, "Don't worry, Bajrang. We will get you to the ADS. We will save you. Just hold on."

He raced into the ADS. The small hospital was known for the skill and dedication of its overworked team of doctors, nurses and attendants, and invariably the best were posted in this conflict zone. He drove up virtually to the Commandant's office, as bearers expertly placed Bajrang on a stretcher. Amar ran to the Commandant – a harassed looking Colonel, eyes and cheeks lined by the months of continual stress in trying to save as many of the injured as they could.

He grabbed him by the lapels, "Sir, my boy, Bajrang. He has been hit. For me. You have to save him."

Colonel Goswami walked up briskly to where Bajrang lay on a stretcher. He did not need to look any closer to know that he had been dead for quite a while. But he lifted the stiffening eyelids, shone a light on the retina, and closed the lids again.

He turned to Amar, "It is too late. He is dead." He spoke clinically, in a quiet impersonal tone. Years of experience had told him that it was best to break the news that way.

Amar grabbed him by the lapels, "How do you know? You didn't even see him properly. Why don't you check his heart? Why don't you at least examine him?"

"Son, I know."

Amar burst out, the anger and frustration spilling out with every word, "You know? What do you know? You guys in the rear sit in your cushy offices, while we are there in the front. What do you know? You lazy bums can't even get your arse up to check us properly."

Colonel Goswami gently removed Amar's hands from his lapels. He was an old wizened doctor who had volunteered to be in the conflict zone. He had seen scenes like this often before. He led Amar to a chair and removed his rifle from his hands. The lifeless body of Bajrang was carried away.

Colonel Goswami watched Amar slumped on his chair and placed his hands gently on his shoulder, "Son, how long have you been here?"

"Thirteen months now. Thirteen months and seven days." He smiled wanly, "When you are here, you count each day."

"You need to rest. Remember, if you are tired or stressed, you could take decisions that could endanger your men."

The tent flap opened and the tall figure of Colonel Sangha burst into the room. His normally gruff face was a mask of worry. Amar stood up involuntarily, and Sangha put a huge hand on his shoulder pressing him back to the seat.

"Amar, I heard about the incident. Are you okay? Are the rest of your men okay?"

Amar nodded wanly. "I lost another man today, Sir. It was my fault."

Sangha gently ruffled his hair. It was a gesture that seemed totally out of place with that gruff, hard-boiled soldier.

"Don't blame yourself for it, Amar. These things happen in action."

"No, Sir. It was my fault. It was because of me. I killed Bajrang. Like I killed Tejpal and Ranjit. It was all my fault." Tears rolled down his cheeks as he recounted it.

Sangha put his huge arms around his shoulders. He let Amar cry, and when he had finished and composed himself, said very gently, "You know, Amar, when I was young like you – yes, it may surprise you, but I too was young once." The weak joke made Amar smile, as he hoped it would. Sangha continued, "I was posted at the Siachen Glacier. I had taken a team to a neighbouring post and as we were returning, one of my boys fell into a crevice. We pulled him out. He had fractured a leg and was in a bad shape. We took turns carrying him. I carried him on my back for half a kilometre. We made a makeshift stretcher and carried him in shifts. But you know how it is at those heights. You can't walk twenty yards without becoming breathless, and it was impossible to carry him any farther. He was slipping and the rest of the boys were getting too exhausted to continue. And there was a storm coming up."

He stopped. The memory seemed to hurt even now, "I made the decision. We left the boy. Put him in a snow cave, marked it, and promised we would come back. We barely made it back to the camp before the storm struck. We could not move out for three days after that, and when we did, we never did find him. His body was never recovered. I blamed myself for his death for months after that. I could see his face in my dreams, pleading not to be left behind. I started drinking heavily. It took me years to recover, and even now I don't know whether I killed that boy, or whether I saved the lives of the other six who were with me."

He paused, "In operations we have to take some very

difficult decisions, Amar. Some may be right; some may be wrong. But you have to trust your judgement and your instincts. It is the man on the spot who has to take that split-second decision. No one else can do it for him."

Amar sat up in his chair while Sangha continued reassuring him, "Don't dwell on the past. Think with a cool mind and don't take things personally. I will ensure that Bajrang's family get all their entitlements and more. You rest now and look after yourself."

He ruffled Amar's hair again, a smile breaking across the big bearded face, "After all, I need my top company commander to be at his best, don't I?"

II

Amar spent the night at the ADS with his team. Colonel Sangha's words were reassuring, but he could not push the image of Bajrang's lifeless body, wearing his bloodied jacket, out of his mind. He returned the next morning to his camp. Sangha had provided another QRT vehicle for additional security and the small column wound its way back to camp. They entered the outskirts of the town and drove down the familiar road that wound its way to his camp. As they did so, a tall *burqa*-clad figure saw him drive past. She paused in mid-stride with surprise, but regained composure and continued walking, keeping her eyes on Captain Amar till his vehicle entered the gates of his camp and disappeared from view.

She rushed back to her home, pulled out her phone and called a number. There was no name attached to it, but she knew it by heart. It was Aurangzeb at the other end. Her heart pounded as she wondered how he would receive the news. After all, she had seen Aurangzeb's anger at close range. She gulped and then blurted out,

"Janaab. Captain zinda hai. Maine use aaj subeh dekha hai" (The Captain is alive. I saw him myself this morning).

"Impossible. I shot him myself. I never miss."

"He is alive, *Janaab*. He was driving his vehicle and going back to his camp. I saw him with my own eyes."

Aurangzeb's face darkened with anger. He picked up his rifle and stalked out, perhaps to find another target on which he could vent his anger on. His aides, Majid and Sajid, came running behind to follow.

He waved them away angrily, "No. I want to be by myself."

"Janaab. It may be dangerous."

He glared at them, "Do as I tell you, wait here. I want to be alone." And then strode away into the thickly wooded mountains in an attempt to cool the anger that was burning inside him.

Aurangzeb Meets Shazia

Aurangzeb walked through the hills alone with his thoughts. The Captain obsessed him. A young titch of a boy, whom he should have swept aside with one blow. Instead, he had attacked his camp, killed his men, killed his contact, Mirwaiz, and damn it, even his own men were talking about what a marksman he was. And to make matters worse, his attempt on Amar had failed. He did not know how; all he knew was that Amar was still alive.

He walked for hours, not feeling the cold, the heat or the exertions. His heavy jacket and jersey turned wet with perspiration in spite of the cold, and it was only then that he realized that he was thirsty.

He looked around. He was in the outskirts of the town and there was no army activity around. The only house in the vicinity was a single-storey wooden house atop a little hillock. There seemed nobody there.

He edged closer keeping to the shadows, till he entered the walnut grove at the base of the hill. Hidden from view, he could see the house clearly. It was a typical Kashmiri house, made of wood and brick, and capped with long sloping roofs. A small barn stood next to it with chickens and goats scrabbling around a low metal trough that held their feed. Adjoining it was a well with a low-parapet wall around it , with a single pulley at the edge.

She was drawing water from the well, pulling up the bucket of water from its depths. He watched her smooth fluid motions. And then she tilted her face to wipe her forehead and he saw her face.

He recognized her, of course. He never forgot a face – that was one of his hallmarks. In any case, one could never forget so beautiful a face. She was that teacher he had seen at Umar Husseini's rally, and then again when she frantically poured water over the flames of her burning school – the school he himself had set ablaze.

He adjusted his *keffiyeh* scarf around his face, looked around in a final reconfirmation of the area, and walked up to the well. As always, he moved silently like a panther, and was behind the girl before she even realized it. It was only when his shadow fell on her that she became aware of his presence and looked up with a start.

He gestured towards the house. "Who is in there?"

"No one. Just me and my parents."

"Any Indian dogs around?"

She shook his head, "No *Janaab*."

"You? Who are you?"

"Shazia. Shazia Junaid."

"*Paani*"

She pulled up the bucket, spilling most of it in her fear and poured the water directly from the bucket into his open palms. He drank deeply, running it over his hair and neck, wetting the edges of his *keffiyeh* scarf to wipe his eyes and forehead, and then stood up looking directly at her.

"Shukhriyan. Yahan ka paani bahut meetha hai."(Thank you. The water here is very sweet).

He reached out for her and traced his finger across her cheek. She stiffened and recoiled, her body burning with his touch.

He ran his finger from her cheek to her lips, let it run down to her neck, lingered for a while, then withdrew his hand and smiled. "*Bilkul tumhare tarah." (*Just like you).

Aurangzeb disappeared into the shadows as silently as he had appeared. Shazia ran back to her house, closing the flimsy door and bolting it. Her mother rushed up to her, sensing the fear.

"Beti, kya hua? You look like you have seen a ghost."

"Not a ghost. A demon. I hope I never see him again." She sat down shaken. She did not speak more. She just sat trembling as her mother poured her some *kahwa,* which she sipped in silence. There was something about that man that that terrified her. He had said little, but his eyes held an evil which she hoped she would never see again.

II

She was wrong.

He came back just two weeks later. This time it was in the mid-afternoon. He had selected his time well. Army activity was usually lax in the afternoons and intensified later in the evenings and nights.

He was a little surprised that he had decided to return to her place. He was not the kind of man who took needless risks. That is why he had remained alive so long. He never went back to a place if he could avoid it. But somehow the thought of Shazia and that beautiful vulnerable face seemed to come back to him. It would do no harm to pay a quick visit.

This time he took Sajid and Majid with him. He had moved away from the camp ostensibly to recce the area for his next strike, and no one else knew where he was. But then in any case, he came and went as he pleased. He approached the small house on the hill cautiously, first sending Sajid and Majid ahead to scour the area and ensure that it was clear. He then followed, and took cover in the grove of apple and walnut trees in the small orchard, and signalled them to check the house from within.

The two brothers approached the house with caution. In one swift movement they kicked open the door and entered, their guns covering both sides of the darkened room. They pointed their guns towards Shazia and her parents who were huddled around the small fireplace, in the slowly growing chill. Majid called out, "Any dogs here. Any Army? Is there anyone else here?"

Shazia's father stood up, hands folded, imploring, "No *Janaab*. There is no one else here. Just me, my wife and my daughter. There has been no army here for months."

Sajid ran upstairs and took a quick look at Shazia's small room on the upper storey, while Majid continued covering Shazia and her parents. Only when they were satisfied, did they wave out to Aurangzeb to come in.

He walked in, his frame filled the doorway, his face obscured by his *keffiyeh*. Only his eyes were visible, narrowed and menacing. He walked in and sat by the table.

"Food. Bring us food," he commanded.

Her mother rushed to the kitchen, rustled up some of

the remnants of their lunch of rice and *rajma* and placed a plate before Aurangzeb. He looked at it and sniffed, "What is this? Is this how you treat a guest? Don't you have anything better to give us?"

Majid grinned evilly and walked out of the room. He came back a few minutes later holding two chickens which he had taken from the coop fluttering in his hands. He held them with one large hand, and withdrew a slim dagger from his belt. Then, in a smooth motion, he slit the throat of one, and then the other, and watched with a slightly amused expression as life ebbed out of them. Slowly, they ceased their struggling. He threw them on the floor, "Cook these."

Shazia's mother hastily began cleaning and cooking the chickens. They were the last they had and their eggs were one of the few luxuries still available to them. But she did not protest. With these militants it was best to do exactly what they asked, and just hope that they would go away. She had seen their violence and brutality from close quarters. As she cooked with trembling hands, she prayed, "Allah. Let them take what they want, but don't let them touch my Shazia."

She served out the food in three plates and placed them on the table. Aurangzeb ate first, while Sajid and Majid kept guard at the window. It was only when he had finished that the two brothers began eating, one at a time, with the other kept guard at the window.

Aurangzeb drank the water placed in the cheap aluminium cup before him, and then seemed to relax for the first time. He looked around the house and fixed his gaze intently on Shazia, his eyes taking in the curve of her *firhan*, the swell of her breasts and the paleness of her neck. She was pale with fear, but even then, her beauty shone like a beacon.

Suddenly he asked, "So Shazia. Shazia Junaid. And what do you do?"

She blurted out unthinking, "I am a teacher. I taught in the school."

"Taught in the school? Yes, I know. I saw you there. But what school? I burnt it down myself. I even saw you there when the school was burning."

Shazia continued looking down. It was pointless saying anything to them. Let's hope they just eat and go, she thought to herself.

He walked up to her and placed his hand on her chin. With one finger he raised her face, so that her eyes were on level with his.

"And why do you teach in a school in any case? Don't you know its un-Islamic. And you go out on your own, don't you? Without your father accompanying you? Why?"

Shazia kept quiet. He went on, "You Kashmiris do not know. That is why we are here. To wage *jihad* for you. To get you freedom from these Indian dogs. To teach you the right way of life."

He turned to her father, "And you, old man. Don't you have a son you can give to the *jihad*. Or are you Kashmiris incapable of producing men anymore?"

As he said these cruel words, Shazia's mother hid her face with her scarf. Her eyes welled with tears. Her father looked down for what seemed a very long time. When he finally looked up, his face was streaming with tears, "Yes, I had a son."

Aurangzeb seemed not to notice the effect of his words. He continued, "And where is he then? What happened to him?"

Something snapped in Shazia. She pushed his hand away from her face, and shouted out, "Yes, I had a brother, my Asif. He wanted to start his own taxi service. We were happy. AND THEN YOU CAME!!"

She had shouted out the words, not even aware of the vehemence in her own voice. Her words spilled out, "Yes, you and your kind. Three years ago, when all this talk of *jihad* was in the air, some men came to our village to round up young men. For the *jihad* they said. Some of the youths joined, but Asif refused, once twice, repeatedly. They beat him on the street, and when he fought back, they shot him. Why? Because he did not want to be a part of this. We just wanted to live here in peace." In her anger, her voice had risen to a scream, and her hands flailed against his face and shoulders.

Aurangzeb looked at her, surprised. No one – man or woman – had ever spoken to him like that. He had killed a man who had once merely raised his voice to him. His narrowed eyes filled with menace, as he grabbed her slim hands in one large palm, "You want no part of it. We have come from Pakistan and Afghanistan just to fight for you and you say you want no part of it?"

Majid and Sajid had closed in with their guns levelled. Aurangzeb waved them off, and continued holding Shazia, still glaring at her. Shazia's father came up to him, his hands folded in desperation, "Please *Janaab*. Forgive her. She is a child; she does not know what she is saying." He tried vainly to place himself between them, but Aurangzeb pushed him away with one swing of his powerful arm.

For what seemed an eternity, Aurangzeb continued glaring at Shazia. Then he put his finger on Shazia's chin again, "You have a fire. I like that. I like those with courage." He turned to her father, "I will forgive your daughter now, but remember, if ever you reveal a word to anyone about us, I will not be so forgiving...." He ran a finger across his throat in an unmistakable gesture and let the words hang in the air.

He nodded to Sajid who ran out to see if it was all clear outside. He scanned the area and waved them to come out. Majid followed and took up position on the other side. Then, with his route covered, Aurangzeb strode towards the door to leave. At the entrance he halted suddenly and looked towards Shazia, "You are beautiful and have spirit. But you have much to learn." And like a ghost, he disappeared out of sight.

The family huddled together sobbing in relief and fear, as the door closed behind Aurangzeb. They had a close shave and they knew it. Shazia's outburst could have been fatal for the entire family. And God knows what they would do to Shazia. The militants were known for their treatment of women whom they took as they pleased. Shazia was the first to speak, "We must tell the police and the Army about this. They will protect us."

Her father burst out, "Are you mad? Who will protect us? Don't you know what happened when we went to tell them about Asif? They questioned us as if we were terrorists. If we tell them that *jihadis* had come to our home, they will first put in jail for questioning. And if the terrorists find out that we went to the army, they will come for revenge. God knows what they will do. Be silent over this. It will pass over. Let us just pray they never come back again."

The family cried in the gathering dark as the fire began flickering out behind them. And then silence fell over the valley that seemed to envelop them all.

III

He came back a fortnight later. This time he was alone. His eyes and body language still carried the same cruel menace but this time, his behaviour was not so threatening. He brought a sack containing some rice, rajma, packets of dry fruits and condensed milk. The wrappings had been removed from the tins.

He handed it to her mother, "Keep this. Winter is coming. You will need it."

He sat in silence, as always, his eyes burning through Shazia. She could feel the eyes tearing through her flimsy clothes and revulsion and fear welled up. But surprisingly he did not touch her. He did not even come close to her.

He ate in silence, his eyes fixed on Shazia as she stood trembling, eyes downcast, praying that he would just go away. He finished his meal, and then strode out, disappearing into the night, as the family huddled in their fear.

Shazia broke down, "I can't take this anymore. Whenever he comes, I feel his eyes on my body; it is like he is violating me. I don't know what he will do to me and when."

Her father tried to comfort her, "It will pass my child. Allah will protect us. Maybe he will leave soon. They usually go back to Pakistan after a few months. Till then we can only pray."

He was right. They really had no other option. If they

reported the visit to the Army, they would first question her father as a harbourer, maybe even jail him. And the terrorists would find out about it –they always did. Then their revenge would be fierce. Shazia remembered the brutal manner they had beaten Asif to death just because he had fought back and refused to join them. They had beaten him in the street while not a single person dared lift a finger to help. If they came back for revenge, Shazia would face its brunt. Like so many Kashmiris, they were caught in the vicious battle between the terrorists and the security forces. And more than anyone else, they were its greatest victims.

The Strike that "Will Echo all the Way to Delhi"

Aurangzeb moved back to his hideout at night, avoiding the dragnet of security forces that combed the area. He had been taking far too many chances by visiting Shazia's place so often – and that too alone. It was something he had never done. He had had his share of women, in fact, much more than his share. Some he had taken by force; some had been sent by their families in a gesture of appeasement; others had come willingly. But this one was different. He could take her physically any time he liked, but he knew that by doing so he would lose her completely.

Even as he lay in his sleeping bag at nights, her face and luminous eyes came back to him. He remembered her fire and anger. Why, he would have broken the neck of anyone who dared speak to him like that. He had spared her, and he had not even touched her. He wanted to possess that beautiful, vulnerable woman, and claim her as his in every sense of the term. And that thought sent him back to her place, irrespective of the risks it involved.

He was alone in a bricked building when the call came on his satellite phone. He picked up the phone, *"Janaab?"*

It was Colonel Rashid from across the LOC. As always, he came straight to the point. "Aurangzeb, you have been there long enough. On the next moonless night – three weeks from now – you will cross the LOC into Pakistan. We will cover your move with artillery fire, so that the Indians keep their heads down when you are crossing over."

It was a standard operating procedure. Most ISI operatives usually spent just a season or so in Kashmir, before being pulled back. He had been there for almost a year now. But his work was not over as yet.

"*Janaab.* My role has just begun. I have unfinished work here."

"You have done more than your share, Aurangzeb. You have to get back. But yes, before you return, make one big strike."

Aurangzeb smiled evilly, "I will make another big strike. One that will echo all the way to Delhi. They will tremble at Aurangzeb's name long after I am gone."

Aurangzeb put down the phone, and his mind began ruminating about the big strike he would make. More than the strike, he wanted to kill Amar before he left. He would make the big strike all right, but he would do it in a manner that would eliminate the Captain as well. Two birds with one stone.

As he usually did, he made a detailed reconnaissance of the area till he had gone over it dozens of times and knew each building, each lane, the location of each hut or shepherds' shelter, and each fold of ground on the mountains right up to the LOC. He went around incognito mingling easily with the locals. He wandered around the streets of the small town, along the main road and the bylanes. His eyes took in the shops and the bazaar, the local council building in the centre of the town, the crowded bus station, the police station (now even more fortified after his assassination of S P Altaf, the army camp on the outskirts of the town, and the makeshift camp of migrant labourers that had sprung up adjoining it. Each of these places imprinted itself in the map in his mind and became interconnected as his plan slowly evolved. He meticulously planned a series of strikes – strikes that would draw the big fish. And then the strike on the big fish that would draw Amar as well. He would make that strike right at the gates of Amar's camp, and then kill that bastard as well when he appeared.

The timing would have to be precise though. He would have to make the strike just a day before he crossed the LOC. His move would have to be perfectly synchronized, so that he could get away even as the security forces were reeling in the aftermath of the strike.

And he knew one thing. When he left, he would take Shazia with him.

Shazia Agrees to Help

It had been over a month since Amar's narrow escape, but he still blamed himself for Bajrang's death. The long talk with Colonel Sangha had helped a great deal in restoring his confidence, but he could still not get the ghosts out of his mind. He saw the dead body of Bajrang in his jacket, repeatedly. He remembered the mutilated body of Tejpal and cursed himself for agreeing to his plan to infiltrate Aurangzeb's *tanzeem* – a plan that had ended in such disaster. He could see Ranjit and his buddy fall from the water tower, as he watched helplessly. Not even his successful raid on Aurangzeb's camp could make up for all that. Nor could he forget the grieving widow of SP Altaf – a man who had become a friend with whom they had shared so many difficult moments in the darkest days of the insurgency. The images haunted him, and filled his dreams and caused nightmares. The stress was taking its toll, and in spite of all that Colonel Sangha had told him, it had become a personal vendetta. He had to get Aurangzeb. He would track down that bastard and kill him the same way he had killed Ghazi.

But how? After the attack on Amar, Aurangzeb had maintained a low profile. There had been no other strikes after that. There was no trace of him – no news, no clues, nothing. He was lying low, which meant that something big was in the offing.

Like all military drills, the answer lay in intensifying patrolling and conducting what the army called 'area domination operations.' Amar virtually scoured the entire area without coming across any trace of Aurangzeb or his *tanzeem*. They seemed to have vanished. And now winter was setting in. It would be Amar's second winter in Kashmir and he knew that it usually saw an intensification of activity before it fully set in. The terrorists lay low during the winter months since operations were difficult and they could be tracked in the snow, and most exfiltrated to Pakistan before that. Aurangzeb would do the same. But knowing him, he would want to make one major strike before leaving.

He led his patrols across the town, the mountain reaches, along *nullahs* and likely hiding places, but with little effect. During one of them, he passed by the area of Shazia's house. He had not seen her since the school had burnt down, but knew she stayed there. And when his patrol crossed the small house on the hillock, his gaze lingered on it, hoping to catch a glimpse of her. It was then that his buddy, Sameer, pointed to some unusual footprints on the ground. They were the boot marks of hob-nailed shoes, worn only by the army or terrorists who had been supplied with them by the Pakistanis. They were not the shoes a simple farmer would wear. The footmarks led to a grove at the base of the hill. And there, by a bush were signs of that someone had lain there for a while. These were suspicious marks that indicated an unusual presence and Amar decided to go to the house and have a closer look. He did not know it then, but Aurangzeb had visited the house just the night before.

He walked up to the house taking only Sameer with him. He left the rest of the patrol behind, hidden in cover.

The sight of too many security personnel could be counter-productive. He knew, he was taking a gamble in going there like that, and his heart thumped as walked up from the grove towards the old wooden building.

Shazia's father was tending chickens when Amar came up and greeted him with an air of false cheerfulness, *"Salaam aliekum, miyan."*

He nodded briefly, not replying, and continued feeding the chickens. Years of being caught in the crossfire between the security forces and the militants had left the Kashmiris wary and secretive.

Amar tried to coax him into conversation, "*Ha, anaab. kaise hon?*"

"*Theek hai, Janaab.*"

"Aap ka ghar gaon se kaafi door hai. Kya yahan sab sahi salamat hai?"(Your home seems a little away from the main village. Is everything okay here?)

"Sahi hai, Janaab". The old man shuffled and tried to go away, putting an end to the conversation. Amar followed him. The old man was tense and seemed scared. He was hiding something. Amar continued probing gently, "Are you sure everything is okay? Tell me if there is some problem. I am here to help you."

The old man muttered something, turned around and began walking back towards his house. Amar knew he was striking a chord and persisted, "Tell me. I can help. What is it?"

The old man walked faster, trying to get away. Amar followed him till the doorsteps of the house. "Listen, I know there is something. I can see it in your face. What is it? What is it that is troubling you?"

The old man turned around, desperation on his face, "There is no problem. There is nobody troubling us. And we don't want your help. We will face our troubles on our own."

Amar homed on to the words, "Troubles? What troubles? The militants? Have they been visiting you?"

Shazia's father put his hands up in a gesture of supplication and as he entered his house said, *"Saab, chhodh dijiye hame. Mujhe nahi aap se koi matlab hai, na in ladko se. Ham beech me pisse jaate hai. Agar unko pata chala ki fauji yahan aaye the, to woh hamare peeche pad jayenge."* (Sir, leave us alone. We want nothing to do with you or those men. We are merely caught in between. If they find out the army had come here, they will come after us).

Amar knew he was on to something, "*Kaun peeche pad jayenge*? Terrorists? Have they been coming here?" He followed the old man into the darkened room of his house, hoping to get some clue out of him.

"NO, NO!!!! Nobody has been coming here. Just leave us alone." His wife ran up, putting her arms around her husband in a feeble gesture of support. It was obvious that the old couple was under a lot a strain. Their fear was tangible. They walked into the house and Amar followed them in.

"We know that Aurangzeb and his *tanzeem* have been operating in this area. Have they been coming here? Have you seen them?"

The couple looked up with a start and Amar knew he had hit the mark, "Tell me. We will get him. Help me get him."

The old man turned away, "We know nothing about it. This is not our battle. Just leave us alone. We can't help."

Amar turned away disappointed when a voice came from the top of the stairs, "I will help you."

It was Shazia. She had watched Amar approaching from her room on the upper storey of the house, and had heard him speak to her father. She had been torn over this decision and had pondered over it ever since Aurangzeb had first entered her house. Somehow the sight of Amar speaking earnestly to her father below helped her decide what was to be done. She walked down the steps and repeated, "I will help you."

Her father reached out for her as she came down the steps, "*Beti,* don't get into this. You don't know how dangerous it could get."

"I know. And I am ready for it. We have been living in fear since that man came here, and we know he will come again." She turned to Amar, "I know who you are looking for. He has come here."

Amar turned to her, "Who has come here? Is it Aurangzeb?"

"I don't know who he is. I have never even seen his face properly. All I know is that it is a *shaitan* who comes. An evil man who fills me with terror every time he approaches."

"And you are still ready to help us?"

"Yes. I am ready. We can't live in constant fear like this. We have to stop him. Tell me what is it that you want me to do?"

"I want you to tell me when Aurangzeb comes here next."

"But how will I be able to tell you. He comes and leaves unexpectedly."

Amar took out a watch from his pocket. It was a battered old watch – akin to the one Tejpal had been wearing. "Take it. It is more than a watch. Press this," he pointed to a hidden button beneath its face, "and I will receive a beep and know your exact position on my own device. I will come immediately when I get this message."

She took the watch and put it on. She pressed the hidden switch on the inside of the watch and a soft beep sounded on Amar's own watch. His watch glowed and a GPS coordinate appeared on its face, indicating the location. Amar looked at it with a pang. The last time it had glowed like this was when Tejpal had activated his own device. He had been unable to save Tejpal then. God, what if he made the same mistake with Shazia. The consequences would be much worse.

He nodded, "Shazia, you know he is a dangerous man." He took out his pistol and handed it to her, "You may need this for your protection."

Shazia looked at it with hesitation, unsure of what to do. Amar asked, "Have you ever fired one before?"

She nodded, "No. This is the first time I am even holding such a weapon."

Amar picked up the pistol. "Don't worry. It is not very difficult. I will teach you how to use it." He removed the magazine from the weapon for safety and started his lesson. "To fire it, you have to first cock it like this." He gently cocked it, passed it to Shazia who repeated the action a few times. Amar continued, "And then you shift the safety catch from 'Safe' to 'Fire' position like this." He let Shazia repeat the motion a few times so that she got the feel of it. "And now comes the most important part. Firing it." He lifted the weapon to his right eye, "You take aim with one eye, keeping the sight in the centre of the target and gently squeeze the trigger. Like this." He passed the gun to her, "Try it once."

He gave the weapon to her. She cocked it, closed her eyes and fired, half expecting a violent bang of a shot. There was no live round and the hammer clicked harmlessly. She did it a few times more, each time with growing assurance. Amar smiled, "Okay, that was not bad. Next time we will try with the loaded magazine." He fitted the loaded magazine on the weapon. "Here, it is loaded now. To fire, all you have to do is to cock, unlock the safety catch and press the trigger. And when you take aim to fire, try to keep your eyes open."

He handed the loaded weapon to her. She took it tentatively. Amar smiled, "Don't worry. It won't fire till you press the trigger. Now, hide it someplace safely. I hope you never have to use it, but should you, it will give some protection. *Khuda hafiz.*"

Amar and Iqbal

Amar was feeling better than he had been in weeks as he drove back to camp. He knew the militant who had visited Shazia could be none other than Aurangzeb, or one of his group. There was no other group operating in the area. The fact that Shazia had agreed to help suddenly opened up a whole new avenue for him.

He thought of Shazia, and again he wondered if he was doing the right thing by putting her in danger. If things went wrong, it would be terrible for her and her family. The image of her face and those luminous eyes crossed his mind again. They had seen too much fear and pain already. God, I hope they don't have to go through more.

He was still feeling positive as he drove through the town back to his camp. He waved out to the shopkeepers on the sides of the road. As he passed the tea and provisions shop, Abdullah waved and came running to greet him. Amar stopped his vehicle, looking inside. There, on the counter was Iqbal. His eyes were bandaged as always and over them he had his dark glasses on. As he moved, his actions were slow but deliberate, his hands seeming to move by memory, as he accepted money from a customer, fingered the note to gauge the currency, and then unerringly handed back the exact change. There seemed to be a half-smile on his face, and his body language spoke of a faint sense of pride.

Abdullah came up to him with a smile, offering him a cup of *kahwa*. Amar turned to Iqbal "Ha, Iqbal, I am glad you took my advice and are helping Abdullah. It's not too difficult is it, once you get the knack of it."

Iqbal turned in the direction of the voice, recognizing it, "Yes, Captain *Saab*." The hostility and resentment were still in the voice, but it seemed to have mellowed a little.

People came and went and Iqbal gave each of them their exact change. He spoke out each transaction into his mobile which was on speech-to-word mode and converted it to text immediately, allowing him to maintain a record of each transaction. He also reached out unerringly to each item that was asked for. He had memorized the layout of the store meticulously and had placed each item where he could get it.

Abdullah beamed proudly, "Iqbal now keeps all the records of the store. He has even told me where to keep each item so he can reach out for it. He seems happier now that he has something to do."

Amar smiled as he watched the scene. Iqbal was an intelligent, educated young man, who could have gone far had it not been for the damned terrorism in the valley. Like so many youths, he had just got caught in the cross-fire and paid a heavy price for a momentary lapse.

Amar continued and told Iqbal, "And, by the way, I have some good news for you. I have tied up with a doctor friend of mine in Jammu, who specializes in these kinds of injuries. He has agreed to have a look at you and is confident that he will be able to help you recover your sight." He pulled out his wallet, removed a card and handed it to him. "Go to Jammu. Meet Dr. Vijay Shukla at the Government Hospital. I have spoken to him about you and he will treat you on priority. Go to him." He pulled out a wad of notes from his wallet – all that was in it – and pressed them into Iqbal's hands. "Take this. It will help."

Iqbal held the notes, uncertain of whether he should accept or refuse. Amar pressed his hand insistently. Finally, Iqbal pressed Amar's hand back, in a gesture of gratitude, and gently withdrew his hand, with the small wad of money in it. He turned to Amar, his face reflecting a range of emotions and slowly removed his dark glasses. His eyes were still covered with bandages, and he rubbed his hands against them. When he looked up, the bandage seemed to be damp with tears, "You know *Saab,* I can only differentiate between dark and light. But sometimes even the light hurts my eyes; it feels like needles in the open wounds of my eyes. I pray every day that I will be able to see, but sometimes it is so bad, all I want is for the pain to go away." He pressed Amar's hand again, "Will I be able to see again? Will this pain really stop?"

"Of course, it will. Just meet Dr Shukla. He has treated over a hundred cases like this. He will cure you as well."

"I will go, thank you." He put his glasses back and walked back to the counter.

Amar smiled, glad that he had succeeded in convincing Iqbal, "Well, now that I am here, I cannot leave without picking up something, can I? Give me a packet of biscuits."

"Jaroor Janaab, kaunsa?"

"Any. Okay, make it chocolate chips."

Iqbal muttered and half smiled, "Choco chips, second shelf, top right corner." He reached out to the shelf behind him and the sleeves of his *firhan* slipped down as he raised his hand to get it from the top shelf, but his hands homed on to it unerringly. He brought the packet down and placed it on the counter before Amar. He seemed to be showing off his new found skills.

Amar looked at the biscuit packet that Iqbal had placed before him, his eyes taking in the smiling face, the hands and down to his feet. He took the biscuit packet and handed him a 200-rupee note. Iqbal refused to take the money initially, but Amar insisted. He took the note, ran his fingers over it, then counted out the change and placed it on the counter.

Amar took the change, "Exact." He smiled, put the change and the biscuit packet in his pocket, turned and walked back to his vehicle.

Aurangzeb's Preparatory Strikes

Even as the pre-winter chill began sweeping the valley, Aurangzeb, began putting his plan in motion. He had just a few weeks left in Kashmir, in which he would let unleash a series of events that would resonate long after he had left. Oh, he would leave an impact all right!

He continued making his reconnaissance of the area, mingling with the locals and wandering through the areas he intended to strike. He now knew each road, by-lane and road like the back of his hand, and had meticulously chalked out the route he would take at each stage of the operation. He walked down the main road that wound through the town a dozen times; he followed it as it passed just ahead of Amar's camp, scanning the area beyond it. He climbed up the warren of roofs till he found the perfect position, where he could remain undetected till he made his strike and then be able to get away. The strike would have to be perfectly synchronized and it was dependent on perfect timing and remaining undetected till the last moment.

He selected the perfect position from where he would make his attack. A narrow ledge on a roof, partially covered by a sheet of iron. From here he could see the road as it wound its way past Amar's camp and through the town. Through his binoculars he watched vehicles and army convoys moving in a continual stream down that road, saw the shops that dotted the pavement on the sides, and the migrant labourers camp just a few hundred yards away from the gates of Amar's camp. The labourers from Bihar and Uttar Pradesh had been coming regularly to Kashmir for work in the orchards and rice fields. They had stopped in the worst days of terrorism but were gradually returning again. They were harmless – just trying to eke out a living – but they were an important link in his plan.

He had been hearing announcements made repeatedly in the newspapers and on television about how the situation in Kashmir was fast coming under control after Article 370 had been revoked; how tourists were thronging to the valley in thousands; how peace and normalcy had returned. The Home Minister boasted on television that even the Kashmiri Pundits who had fled in the worst days, were returning now. The Indian government was getting a little too cocky. It needed to be pegged back a little. And what he was planning would do just that.

He would aim for the big fish. And for that, he would need some small fish as bait.

And when the big fish arrived, he would use it to get Amar as well.

He went through his plan repeatedly. And then launched the first phase.

A shopkeeper was just passing a bale of cloth to a customer when a bullet hit him on his head. He was dead even before his body crashed on the counter, and bloodied the bales of cloth strewn over it.

The motor cyclist had halted at a traffic light when a bullet pierced his fragile helmet and shattered his skull. The bullet hit just as the traffic signal turned green. Even as the people behind began honking angrily, he keeled over and fell, his motor cycle falling over him.

The first was Anil Bhat. He had just come back and re-opened his shop in Sopore a few months earlier, hoping to pick up the threads of a life that he had been forced out of. The other was Vikram Kaul, a medical student from Jammu, who had returned for a visit to his old home in the area.

And then the big strike took place.

Kashmir is full of scenic spots where tourist throng to. The natural beauty of the place is so rich, that virtually every turn in the road leads to an exquisite spot, breath taking in beauty. Just a few kilometers from Amar's camp were the scenic Burzdil meadows, a rolling expanse of emerald green with the Sind River flowing through it, and tall pines cresting the low mountain range running alongside it. The place thronged with locals and tourists from across the country and this time it was even more crowded than usual. It was perfect, picture perfect.

Aurangzeb took up position in the upper reaches of the mountains hidden behind cover. There had been no police or army presence in the area for days – perhaps they too were getting lax – and he knew he had time to do what he wanted to do and get away undetected. He watched the noisy throng of people below through his binoculars – men, women, children, the hawkers selling candy floss, peanuts and wafers, the pony handlers leading emaciated ponies with a child or so atop them, and vendors with trinkets and thermos flasks of kahwa. Begum was down there as well, mingling anonymously in the crowd. She would indicate the proper targets and give him advance information should the police or security forces suddenly come to the area.

He waited as he absorbed the scene below. Begum walked around, halting briefly by the side of random groups. He knew what that meant. They were the targets he had to hit. They had to be tourists, from outside the state. Then the message would really hurt. And they were easy to distinguish from the locals with their dress and manner. He identified around eight of them carefully through his scope, and tracked their movements as he waited for the perfect shot. And then he fired. Once, twice, thrice.... emptying his magazine in ten perfectly aimed shots that hit six of them, and dropped them to the ground, their blood turning the green around them to a dark red. He saw the women screaming and running up to the fallen bodies, he heard the sounds of wailing increase, and saw the panic below, and people fled back, not comprehending what was happening. He watched the confusion with a satisfied smile, then withdrew his rifle, collected the empty cartridge cases around him so as to leave no trace of his presence, and the melted away across the mountains to his secret hideout.

II

Amar stood at attention as Colonel Sangha chewed him out. "Six of them, all tourists, and we had four locals killed the week before. And all in your area of responsibility. All killed by a nameless terrorist and you have no idea about it." He waved a newspaper in Amar's face. "Can you see what this says. It says that Kashmir is slipping back to the old days. It says that minorities are being targeted again. They are calling for the Home Minister's resignation. Damn it, they have asked questions in Parliament about it."

Amar waited for the tirade to subside, "Sir, it was not a unknown terrorist. It was Aurangzeb."

"Aurangzeb? But why would he want to hit these targets. He usually goes in for high- profile killings."

"Sir, it is part of a plan. See his *modus operandi*. A single shot in the head. It is Aurangzeb all right."

Sangha looked thoughtful, "Maybe you are right. Why did he go after these labourers? What can he achieve by it?"

"Sir, they are changing tactics. They are hitting people at random to make them leave. They know these soft targets can't be protected."

"But it has created an uproar in Delhi and the rest of the country all right. The Union Minister of State is coming here on Saturday for a high-level meeting of police, military and civil administrations to take stock of the situation. His security is our responsibility. Check everything. Sanitize the entire area. We cannot afford to take any chances."

Amar looked thoughtful and then said, "I will do that, Sir." He had a faint idea what Aurangzeb's plan could be, and how he would go about doing it. And also, what he had to do to stop it.

The Attack on the Minister

Over the next few days, preparations were made for the visit of the Minister of State. The Army and police sanitized the area, checked the culverts for IEDs, and even cleared the undergrowth on both sides of the road. Amar supervised it himself. The route by which the Minister would go for his meeting in the town, passed through his area of responsibility and he would be personally accountable for its security.

Aurangzeb was making his own preparations for the visit and the strike he had in mind. He crouched behind an open window observing the army and security forces milling around. As always, their response was to flood the area with troops hoping to thwart any likely attack. Good. That would add to the confusion. His mind replayed the one shot that would ring all the way to Delhi. And the next shot that would get the Captain. Two birds with two carefully timed shots.

Aurangzeb went around, incognito, as always, for one final reconnaissance. He had merged so completely with the locals that no one noticed him now. He saw the position he would take, and the one to be taken by his back-up team comprising Sajid and Majid. There would be no one else. Of course, Begum would serve as his spotter and give him advance information as she always did. She had been invaluable for him, but he would have to finish her off as well before he left. He could leave no trace of his presence behind.

He knew what he would do. He would hit the Minister right in front of Amar's camp. It would have to be done at a much longer range than usual – almost 900 yards, but he was confident he would be able to do it. He had struck targets as far as 1100 yards in Afghanistan. Ironically, the army had cleared the undergrowth and trees around their camp for their own security and that now gave him a clear field of view. Hitting so close to the camp would draw Amar there, where he could also be engaged and killed.

He had selected a rooftop – no different from the hundreds of rooftops in the small town – which gave him a clear view of the entire area, and a perfect field of fire. From there he could see the approaching road, Amar's camp by its side, even the town itself. That position also provided some overhead cover that would conceal him from the drones that would be hovering overhead. Most importantly, it provided an escape route that would give him a concealed withdrawal after he had made his shot. Begum would be in her position, relaying the news of the Minister's movements, and the activity of the security forces. Majid and Sajid would be in position a few hundred yards to his right – hidden in another warren of roofs. They were to act as a back-up, but their main role was to draw out the Army which would retaliate immediately after the first shot, and divert them away from him.

The difficult part would be the getaway. For that, his disguise would help. No one would suspect him. He would just mingle with the local population in the confusion and disappear in their midst. And then, he would slip through the thickly wooded mountains and cross the LOC. But before he did so, he would have to make a dangerous detour. He would stop at Shazia's home and carry her back with him. He was determined to have her, in spite of the risks involved.

II

Even as Aurangzeb was making his preparations, Amar was making his. He had sanitised both sides of the road, and had positioned his men all along. A road-opening party had been deployed in the wooded hills around. Aurangzeb could fire from anywhere at long range, but Amar felt he had a good idea as to where the shot would come from. However, to prevent that shot and detect and kill Aurangzeb, he would have to go alone – maybe just with Sameer – so they could catch him by surprise. If Aurangzeb detected a large number of troops around him, he would just lie doggo and disappear. And then they would never find him.

That morning, He drove along the road lined with shops for one last check, telling them to down their shutters. It was standard operating procedure. The shops along a VIP route were invariably closed during movement such as this. It made it easier to manage.

One of the shopkeepers called out. "*Saab, aaj bahut bandobast hai. Suna hai koi bada officer ane wala hai*" (Sir, there is a lot of activity. Seems like a big officer is coming).

He waved back to him, "*Bas, jyada nahi hai. Aap ko apni dukaan thode der ke liya band karna padega.*" (Don't worry. You will have to close your shops for a short while. Not much).

He passed Abdullah's tea shop. He came running when he saw Amar and kissed his hand. "*Janaab, shukhriyan, shukhriyan.*"

'What happened?"

"Iqbal has taken your advice. He has gone to Jammu to see the eye doctor. l put him on the bus myself and told my uncle's son to receive him there." He kissed his hands again, "I hope it works."

Amar smiled, "I am sure it will. I will speak to Dr. Shukla and follow up on it. But now all of you get inside, close down your shop and keep the road clear." He drove past the main road watching the shutters closing down and the road being cleared and hoped that he had not miscalculated.

He spent the next few hours checking and rechecking each of his positions, ensuring radio communication and mutual support. Drones hovered overhead along the sides of the road; soldiers and policemen seemed to be behind every tree. Amar drove up and down the road repeatedly, hoping he had covered every contingency – especially the main one.

The radio set buzzed. It was Colonel Sangha, "Amar, Hotel is approaching your AOR. Are your men in position?"

"Yes, Sir. I am here too. We are ready."

"Roger. Keep me abreast of all that is happening. Good luck."

Amar scanned the road along which the Minister would be coming. He had placed his QRT which would take over when the Minister's cavalcade approached his area of responsibility, and then lead the way. The radio buzzed again. It was the JCO in charge of the QRT *"Saab, apne area main aa gaye hain. Main unhe lead kar raha hoon."* (He has entered our area. I am leading the way).

Amar looked at his watch. It would take around 30 minutes for the convoy to reach the town. Along the road, army vehicles raced past, clearing the road, and ensuring that there was no undue movement. Their actions were watched by the tall *burqa*-clad figure who was in position on a open terrace, overlooking the road. She whispered into her satellite phone, *"Ane wala hai."*

Aurangzeb received the message lying on a rooftop covered with a sniper cloth; he was barely visible. He was lying in a narrow space on roof, with a thin sheet of asbestos covering him. His face was covered by his *keffiyeh*, *Badr* was cradled against his shoulders, loosely held in one hand, while his usual *taweez* twirled around the fingers of the other. Through his scope he scanned the road down which the Minister's convoy would come.

Amar got a message from his QRT JCO, *"Saab, Check point 1 cross kar liya. Tees minute main pahunch jayenge."* (We have crossed check point 1. We will reach in around 30 minutes)

"*Taiyar hon. Pata hain nah, kya karna hai?"* (Be ready. You know what to do).

"*Haan Saab.*"

"Okay. I am going in now."

Amar jumped off his vehicle, which sped away in the opposite direction. He raced back towards the town on foot with only Sameer accompanying him, weaving his way through the deserted back streets till he came to the back of Abdullah's shop. Slowly he pushed the door open and entered. The shop was empty as he had expected and no one was visible. He climbed up the stairs, pistol in hand and opened the door leading to the terrace – just a crack – and peered out. On the roof was a burqa-clad figure, watching the scene below through binoculars, speaking into a satellite phone. "He seems to be coming closer now. The Army activity is increasing now."

The message was received by Aurangzeb in his hiding place on the roof. He adjusted his scope and fingered his *taweez*. "Around 10 minutes more, *Badr,* be patient. We will add a big one to your tally."

On the roof, Amar closed in towards Begum who was still focused on the road. He yanked her by the back of her neck, grabbed the satellite phone to prevent any transmission, and pinned her to the ground.

He yanked the *burqa* revealing the face beneath it. It was not a woman.

It was Abdullah.

"I knew it was you." He held Abdullah by the throat and shook him roughly. "Where is Aurangzeb? Where is that bastard, tell me. You have been passing information to him, haven't you?" He slapped him hard.

Abdullah lay on the ground absorbing the blows. "I don't know where he is, I promise. I only do what he tells me to do. I don't know where he is. Please believe me. I did not want to do any of this. He forced me. He threatened to kill my family. Please believe me."

Amar slapped him hard, twice, thrice...repeatedly, "Tell me where is Abdullah. And I may still forgive you. You know where he is."

Abdullah continued pleading, covering his face with his hands to stop the blows, "I don't know. I swear. I promise you...." His words stopped suddenly, as he broke into a paroxysm of coughing and then his body seemed to stiffen in Amar's hand. He jerked once, twice, seemed to have one large convulsion and then fell lifeless at Amar's feet.

He was dead. The tell-tale frothing around the mouth revealed that like Doctor Mirwaiz earlier, he too had crunched on a cyanide pill.

Amar looked at the lifeless body on the ground., "That bastard will not tell us anything now. But Aurangzeb has to be somewhere nearby. But where...?"

Amar took position on the roof and scanned the area with his sniper scope, systematically covering each house, each roof top, each likely hiding place, for any sign of suspicious activity. In that warren of roofs, Aurangzeb could be any place. He could also be inside one of the houses, watching and waiting for the right moment to fire. Amar laid down his scope and scanned the area with his binoculars, "We don't have much time now. The Minister is approaching."

In his concealed hiding place, Aurangzeb saw the convoy approaching. He focused on a spot near the main gate of the army camp and took aim at a spot where the Minister's cavalcade would pass. Slowly, he started intoning a prayer, *taweez* in hand, whispering to his weapon as if it was a living person.

Amar continued scanning the area in desperation. It was too late now. He had not been able to detect Aurangzeb. He had to stop the Minister from coming too close. But he had prepared for this contingency as well. He radioed his QRT vehicle leading the Minister's convoy. "Okay Saab. Now."

The Minister's cavalcade came into view. It turned the corner of the hill and approached a level stretch of road near Amar's camp. Aurangzeb adjusted his focus, as he followed the path of the convoy – a QRT vehicle leading, followed by a police car, then a white Ambassador with tinted glasses in which the Home Minister would be travelling, and followed by another QRT vehicle, ambulance and back-up vehicle in the rear. He focused on the rear side window of the Minister's car. Even through the tinted glass he could make out the figure inside. He increased the magnification of his sniper scope and the head came clearly in view. His intonation increased and he was all set to press the trigger at the right moment when ...

The leading QRT vehicle suddenly veered to the left, towards the main gate of the army camp whose gates opened in a pre-determined move. The entire convoy turned into the camp, the gates closed, and the vehicles disappeared from view.

"Bloody hell!!" Aurangzeb pounded his fist, "Where did he go." He continued training his sights on the closed gate. Just a few moments more and he would have got the perfect shot.

From his position, Amar continued scanning the roofs, hoping to see the elusive Aurangzeb. His radio crackled. It was Colonel Sangha, "Amar, what is going on? Has the Minister crossed your area yet?"

Amar gulped, "Sir, he has entered my area, But I halted the convoy and took him into my camp. I detected a likely attack on him. Am just re-checking before I let them pass."

Sangha exploded, "Why the hell did you not check it earlier?"

Amar pleaded, "I did, Sir. I just need to hold him for around twenty minutes or so, till I reconfirm. We can't take a chance."

Sangha growled, "Twenty minutes. And if anything happens, heads will roll. Starting with yours. Twenty minutes, that's all."

III

Inside the camp, Amar's JCO, Om Prakash went up to the Minister's car, saluted, and held the door open as he helped him out. The Minister smiled, shook hands warmly and asked, "Why have I been brought here? My meeting was in the Town Hall."

The JCO smiled apologetically, "Sorry Sir, we received info of a likely threat to your life. We brought you into our camp to keep you safe till we check it."

"Very well. Let me meet your boys and have a cup of tea with them. But twenty minutes, that is all. Then I must be going."

Out on the rooftops, the two snipers continued their cat-and mouse game. Aurangzeb had his eyes trained on the gate, waiting for the car to drive out. Amar still scanned the rooftops, unable to see Aurangzeb.

The Minister mingled with the soldiers, inquired about their welfare and chatted easily. He drank tea from an enamel mug with them, and ate *shakarparas* and oily *bhajiyas* – the standard fare of a company cook house. He hoped someone would be taking photos of him there. It would add tremendously to his image. He waited for twenty minutes or so and then looked at his watch and said, "*Saab*, I thank you for your hospitality. But now I must be going."

The JCO looked appealingly, "*Saab*. We have not been able to clear the threat. Please wait till we do. It could be dangerous."

The Minister smiled, "*Saab,* the entire district administration is waiting for me in the town. If they feel that I am too scared to travel, how will I be able to inspire them? I will take my chances. Thank you for your tea and hospitality." He started walking towards the car.

The JCO looked around worriedly and called Amar on his radio set, "Minister *Saab* insists on leaving. I can't stop him."

Amar knew that would happen, "Okay. Activate our plan."

From his sniper scope Aurangzeb saw the doors of the camp open. He trained his gun on the gate as the QRT vehicle came out, followed by the rest of the convoy. He turned his sights at the Minister's white car. Through the side windows, he could see the white clad figure reclining against the back seat.

In the five seconds he had to make the shot, Aurangzeb zeroed in on the bobbing head in the rear seat, held it in his crosshairs for an instant, and fired. The bullet shattered the windscreen and the figure was hurled sideways with the impact. Yet, rather than halt, the vehicles almost immediately turned around and sped back into the camp, where the gates closed almost instantly behind them. That reaction was too fast, almost as if they had been expecting it and had rehearsed for it. Normally, the vehicles would have halted and people would have milled around in confusion.

Aurangzeb looked up from his sniper scope. He knew

his shot had found its mark. But the shot had also given away Aurangzeb's position. It was just a brief flash, but it was enough for Amar to home in on to the location and identify it. It was almost 500 yards to his right, so beautifully selected that it would not be noticed even if one peered directly at it. His sniper scope focused on the spot and homed in on the prone figure of Aurangzeb.

Even as Aurangzeb removed his eyes from his sniper scope, he detected an unusual movement from the direction of Amar's camp. From the back gate, a column of three vehicles emerged and drove away at breakneck speed. And then he understood what had happened. He had been tricked. The Minister was being whisked away through the rear gate, and he had fired at a decoy. He jerked involuntarily at the realization, and that movement saved his life.

Amar had been watching through his scope. There was very little of Aurangzeb to aim at, he was so perfectly covered, yet he fired. And even as he did so, Aurangzeb jerked aside. His bullet missed by inches and slammed into the wooden parapet by his side. Before Amar could fire again, Aurangzeb vaulted over the parapet wall, landed on a ledge, and jumped into the street below, disappearing from view. Majid and Sajid, who had been on a roof a few hundred yards away, jumped down as well, and the three raced through the narrow streets and back lanes in the gathering dark.

Back in the camp, the Minister's convoy had returned inside. The rear window of the Minister's car was shattered but there is no other damage. The JCO opened the back door, and a spray of shattered glass fell on the body lying in the back seat. But it was not a corpse; it was a mannequin, dressed in the customary white jacket of the Minister. The plastic head was shattered, and had been torn apart from the rest of the body by the impact. There was no other damage. Behind the camp, three vehicles raced away from the gates. In the middle one, sitting between two soldiers, was the Minister, wearing an army jacket and a slightly bemused expression on his face. He did not know how narrowly he had escaped death, but he hoped his secretary would have noted all the details in his diary. It would look good in his memoirs.

Final Confrontation

Aurangzeb and his two men ran through the streets. Though his face was covered by his trademark scarf, his eyes were visible, burning with anger. His plan for a grand strike had come apart. He had been fooled by a chit of a boy and had been unable to get the Minister. The entire area would be swarming with soldiers soon, and he had to get away before it was too late.

He knew the town backwards and led them through the warren of streets, narrow lanes orchards and courtyards of the houses, crossed the town and raced towards the heavily wooded foothills. He would be safer there, and would be able to escape under cover of the night towards the Line of Control. Colonel Rashid would be expecting him to cross over and they would open fire across the LOC to provide cover for him.

They ran deeper into the wooded hills when his satellite phone rang, "Aurangzeb, what happened?" It was Colonel Rashid.

"We couldn't get the bastard. I have to get back now. The Army is all around."

Rashid paused, "We have made arrangements to help you cross the LOC. Just get there fast. If you don't make it tonight, it may be too late."

It was a moonless night and though the Indian troops

on the LOC would have been alerted by the attempted attack in the town, it was physically impossible to cover every gap along the LOC. And he knew the area well enough to be able to cross even on a pitch-dark night. He would be able to reach the safety of the other side. But before he crossed over, there was something he had to do. He may have failed in getting Amar or the Minister, but he would take Shazia with him.

"Come with me," He ran towards the direction of her house. It was a little away from the direction he had to take, and would cost him an hour or so, but it was a chance he was willing to take. His two men ran with him, panting with effort. Aurangzeb ran like a man possessed, his scarf fluttering behind him, his rifle held in readiness.

The three ran towards the house, stopped and peered around. There was no sign of any untoward movement. He turned to Sajid, "You remain on guard here. We will go in."

Sajid took up position in the walnut grove adjoining the house, while Aurangzeb and Majid crept up. They checked the vicinity once more, kicked the door open and burst in. Shazia's parents were sitting on a carpet next to a small fire. As they stood up with a start, Majid herded them with the barrel of his gun against the wall.

Shazia was in her room upstairs when she heard the sounds below. She rushed out, saw the tall figures with rifles pushing her parents to a side, and instantly knew that her worst fears had come true. She stood hesitatingly at the top of the stairs, when Aurangzeb saw her, "Come down here. You are coming with me."

The terror at seeing Aurangzeb was heightened by the impact of his words. She knew what it meant and she had to gain time. She walked down two steps and then stopped, "Can I get my shawl at least. It will be cold outside." She climbed up the steps slowly back to her room, and grabbed a thick *firhan* and a shawl. As she did so she pressed down on the clasp of the watch that Amar had given her, activating the hidden switch beneath the dial. Then she turned and began walking slowly down the steps, her heart pounding, as Aurangzeb's slanted eyes followed her every move.

Amar had raced after Aurangzeb along with his buddy, Sameer. He had managed to send a radio message to Colonel Sangha telling him that the strike had been averted, and another one to his JCO telling him to follow him with his men. But for now, he was alone with Sameer. The two of them ran blindly through the warren of streets in the congested town, trying to follow the direction that Aurangzeb might have taken. It was hopeless. Aurangzeb could have turned into any street; could have gone anywhere; he could have entered any house; any street could be an ambush site. He knew the danger he was taking, but in his mad chase he threw caution to the winds, as he ran frantically hoping to catch Aurangzeb.

His headlong pursuit had taken him to the very edge of the town, and there was still no trace of Aurangzeb. His men had not caught up with him. He looked around hopelessly for a sign, when his watch face glowed once, and beeped. He stopped with a start, as he realized what it meant. He turned to Sameer. "I know where he is. Come with me, quick." And they ran in the direction of Shazia's house.

Even as they ran, the first flakes of snow began falling around them, melting as they touched their warm hands and faces. Winter had set in early that year.

II

Shazia moved slowly down the stairs, with Aurangzeb watching each move menacingly. Majid's gun was still pointed at her parents, who cowered in a corner. He watched till she came down and then grabbed her with his powerful hands, yanking her close. He turned to her parents, "We are leaving. And I am taking her with me. Do not worry. I will look after her well, and ensure that you too will be well provided. Don't say a word about what you have seen. Remember, your daughter is with me."

Her mother let out a low scream and ran towards Shazia, only to be brutally pushed back by Majid. A cruel blow with his rifle hit her father in the stomach, forcing him to gasp for breath as he collapsed to the ground. Shazia struggled futilely against Aurangzeb's iron grip. She tried to bite him, her teeth sinking into his hands deep enough to draw blood. Aurangzeb barely seemed to notice it, as he dragged her towards the door.

Outside, Amar and Sameer had come near the house; they were in the thickly wooded grove at the base of the hill on which the house stood. In the dark, moonless night Amar could see the silhouette of the wood-and-brick building and its sloping roof. He could make out the small barn, where they had stored their hay for the winter; and the low parapet of the well; and a long metal rectangular trough which they used to feed their animals. He knew Aurangzeb was there. But who else was with him.

The first snowfall of the season had begun. The two men lay in silence as snow flakes began falling around them and contemplated their next move. Sameer nudged him and pointed. There on the other side of the grove, he could make out the figure of Sajid, shuffling in the dark, as he tried to keep warm in the growing cold. It was the sentry Aurangzeb had posted outside. It was fortunate that they had seen him before he saw them. Else he would have sounded the alarm and it would have been all over.

However, they could not move ahead without him seeing them. Sameer, raised his hand to his lips, pulled out his commando dagger, and crawled towards the sentry. Their only chance was to silence him before he raised an alarm.

As Sameer crawled away in the darkness, Amar took position in the wooded grove at the base from where he could see the house. In the darkness, only a single light illuminated the room, visible through the window. He could see nothing but the lit window and a bit of the empty room beyond. He had no idea what was happening inside. He only knew that Aurangzeb was there with Shazia. If he discovered that Amar had come, he would kill Shazia and her parents without a qualm.

Amar lay in the darkness and took aim at the window, hoping that Aurangzeb would show himself there, even if fleetingly. In the inky darkness around him, Sameer crawled through the densely wooded grove, heading for Sajid. He reached close, still undetected, crawled a few yards more, and then another yard, till he was within striking range. Sajid seemed to sense something. He was fidgety and looked around in the dark. Then as he turned to peer in the other direction, and Sameer lunged forward, placed one wiry forearm around his opponent's neck, and tried to stab Sajid before he could make a sound. The two men grappled in the dark in a brutal fight to death.

Inside the house, Aurangzeb was still dragging Shazia towards the door. In the struggle, the sleeve of her *firhan* rose, revealing her wrist and the simple watch on it. Aurangzeb's eyes narrowed, and his anger seemed to smoulder through the layers of his *keffiyeh* covering his face. He raised one hand to her throat, and with the other yanked the watch off her hand, "I killed an informer who was wearing the same kind of watch. How did you get it?" Aurangzeb threw it into the fire and reached for her throat with both hands. Shazia screamed in pain and fear as his grip tightened like an iron vice; Shazia was losing consciousness. In desperation, her hand reached for the scarf around his face . She pulled at it, and just then, a shot rang out in the dark. Aurangzeb loosened his grip for an instant as he looked up. Almost instantly, another shot followed that smashed the single light and plunged the room into darkness.

III

As Shazia struggled with Aurangzeb in her dimly-lit hut, Sameer and Sajid were engaged in a brutal battle outside. Sameer rammed his entire hand in his adversary's mouth to prevent him from shouting out, and Sajid bit hard. The blood ran from Sameer's hand on to Sajid's face and lips, but he maintained the pressure preventing him from calling out. Slowly, Sameer forced Sajid down and pressed his dagger towards his heart. The sharp point of the commando dagger penetrated the coarse woollen shirt and vest, broke through the skin and entered his chest. Sajid's struggles intensified as he tried to break free. He reached desperately for his gun. But Sameer did not let up. The dagger penetrated deeper towards Sajid's heart, and Sameer jerked it upwards with a twist, bringing on a paroxysm of bloody coughing. But, with the life ebbing out of him, Sajid reached for his rifle and in a final burst of strengt pressed the trigger. Even though the sound of the shot was muffled a little by the bodies, it roared through the silent night like a thunderclap. That shot ripped through Sameer's stomach, slumping him over the dead body of his opponent. The two lay there, as the snow began accumulating over their motionless bodies.

Amar could hear the sounds of scuffling within the house as Aurangzeb grabbed Shazia. He heard Shazia scream and through the dimly-lit window caught glimpses of Aurangzeb and Shazia fleetingly. But he knew it would be futile to try and enter. Aurangzeb would just kill Shazia. He continued training his sights at the lone window, when a shot rang out. It was Sajid's shot – his last act before Sameer killed him. The sound of the shot would have alerted Aurangzeb and surprise was now lost. He had to act now. Instinctively, he aimed at the single bulb visible through the window and fired, shattering it and plunging the room into darkness.

Aurangzeb turned towards where the shot had come from, and Shazia saw her chance. In the dark, she wrenched free with a desperate effort and bolted out through the open door. She ran towards the barn and hid inside it. Aurangzeb and Majid jumped out through the side window and dived for cover behind the low parapet of the well near the house, and the feeding trough adjoining it. Hidden behind cover, Aurangzeb, gently removed a stone from the crumbling wall of the parapet so that he could place his rifle through it and observe without being seen.

Amar switched on his night sights. Aurangzeb had done the same. The snow was falling in gentle flakes now, as the two snipers scanned the area, waiting for the other to make the first move. Amar's sights saw the low parapet of the well, the long metal trough used to feed animals, and the barn behind. They could be behind any of them. His only advantage was that he knew the general area where they were. His own position was still unknown – or so he hoped.

Amar noticed a movement near the well but did not fire. Instead, he picked a stone and in a clean, smooth motion lobbed it towards the well. It hit the metal bucket on the edge sending it clattering down the depths, where it fell with a splash.

The jittery Majid half rose at the sound to fire but Aurangzeb pulled him down with a hiss, "You fool. That's exactly what he wants us to do. Fire and reveal our position."

He too needed to make the Captain reveal his position. He hissed out to Majid. "Remove your cap. Put it on a stick and move it slowly." Majid took off his flat Afghan cap, placed it on a stick and slowly raised it over the parapet. From his hiding place, Amar saw it appear and trained his sights on it. The cap moved gently from side to side. His finger was on the trigger, but he held his fire.

It was the oldest trick in the book, and he was not going to fall for it.

Behind the wall, Majid shifted position, moved his cap again, and then put it back on his head. He knew that the Captain had not fallen for it. He crouched under cover. The snipers waited in darkness, with snow falling gently around them for what seemed hours. No one was willing to make the first move and give away their position.

Then Aurangzeb whispered, "The right edge of the grove, there. He is there. I see him."

Majid peered in the direction Aurangzeb indicated, "Where? I can't see anything."

"There, you fool. Behind the bush in the right corner. Fire there."

Majid knew that he was being set up to reveal his position. He hesitated. Aurangzeb turned his gun towards him. "Do as I say or I will shoot you myself."

Majid crawled to the edge of the parapet and fired a burst. It was a long, un-aimed burst, more for effect than for anything else, and he had exposed himself for less than five seconds. It was enough. A single flash emerged from the grove and Amar's bullet hit him squarely on the chest killing him instantly.

Aurangzeb now saw what he was looking for. He fired at the flash. The bullet hit the sniper scope of Amar's rifle, ricocheted off it, and hit Amar's left forearm. He dropped his gun in pain and shock, let out a muffled cry, but had the presence of mind to immediately pick up the gun and crawl away to another position where, fortunately, he was not seen. He examined his damaged scope. It was bent with the impact of the shot; its lens had shattered, and hung to the rifle by one single screw. Amar yanked the damaged scope free, and placed it on the ground. It was of no use now. Painfully, he cocked his rifle with one hand. Luckily the weapon still worked. It could fire, but without the scope and its night vision lens, he would not be able to shoot with pinpoint accuracy.

He crawled away, trying to move to another position, where he would be able to close in on Aurangzeb's flank or rear. The thickly wooded grove provided cover, and though Aurangzeb scanned the forest with his scope, he remained undetected. But he now held the advantage over

Amar, who had no sniper scope or night vision, and would have to shoot through open sights.

In the deadly duel between the two sworn enemies, Shazia had been momentarily forgotten. She had fled to the barn and was hiding there. She heard the occasional shot outside. And then more silence. She had little idea of what was going on, but as she regained her composure, she remembered the pistol that Amar had given her, which she had hidden in a corner of the barn. With trembling hands, she removed it from its plastic bag, held it gingerly, and tried to recall Amar's instructions. She fitted the loaded magazine clip to the gun, and heard it click as it fitted into place. She cocked it – with a little difficulty – and then looked at the safety catch. Slowly she pressed it down to the 'live' position. As Amar had said, that was all she had to do. The gun was ready to fire now. But she still had to fire it, something she had never done before.

She peeped out of the barn. In the inky darkness outside, she could see little, but the gently falling snow. Then a movement behind the parapet of the well caught her eye. It was Aurangzeb hiding there, his back to her. He seemed to be tracking something on his sniper scope and knew that it would be Amar out in the grove somewhere. In his position, Aurangzeb was virtually invisible. She had to give out his position, but how?

She went back to the barn and took a matchbox. With fumbling hands, she lit a bale of hay, using the burning sticks to set other bales ablaze. The hay caught fire rapidly, and spread to the rafters and sides of the hut. In minutes, the entire hut was in flames, forcing her to run out coughing and gasping as the orange glow of the flames spread across the night.

The glow illuminated Aurangzeb briefly, silhouetting him starkly as he tried to move to where he would not be seen. He was visible for less than an instant, but Amar now knew where he was. But without sights, he would have to get closer to hit his target. He tried to crawl to a position from where he would be able to fire better, and as he did so, his own movement was seen by Aurangzeb. He homed in on the greenish white image of Amar through the night vision device of his scope and tracked the image as it appeared and disappeared, getting in and out of cover. The image disappeared behind a mound of earth, and as he waited for it to reappear, he fingered his *taweez* for the perfect moment to fire.

The figure of Amar appeared momentarily again, and he gently began squeezing the trigger, intoning to *Badr,* a single shot rang out. But it had not come from Aurangzeb; it had been fired by Shazia. The bullet whizzed past his head, missing him narrowly, as it slammed into the low wall behind which he was crouched for cover, sending chips of stone and brick spraying into his face and blinding him momentarily.

He jerked around, turned his rifle around to where the shot had come from. He saw Shazia framed against the burning barn, her face taut with tension, her pistol still pointed towards him. He turned to fire at her, and as he did so, he rose slightly and gave Amar the one shot he had been waiting for. Amar fired almost without conscious aim, and the round hit Aurangzeb in the chest, sending him crashing to the ground.

Shazia was watching, her eyes wide, her mouth open. She looked like she was going to scream, and Amar lifted his hand reassuringly gesturing to her to remain where she was. For what seemed an eternity the players remained frozen where they were, silhouetted by the flames of the burning barn, as flakes of snow fell around them. Amar slowly approached the body, very carefully, very cautiously, his gun pointed towards it with every step. The dreaded terrorist was indeed dead; it was obvious to one who had seen combat. But he was taking no chances. He closed in to the body, lying on its back, the scarf covering most of his face, with only his half-open eyes visible. Near his heart, a small stain had formed. He had obviously died instantly.

Shazia came up to him and he held her comfortingly. From the corner of his eyes, he could see her parents holding each other near the door of their home, still in shock and scared to move closer. Amar held Shazia as they moved closer to the body. He prodded it once, twice, and then using the muzzle of his gun, pulled the scarf away from the face, revealing it for the first time.

It was Iqbal.

Shazia gasped, "It is Iqbal, the blind man. Abdullah's nephew. But how...."

"He was no nephew. He had come from the other side. Nor was he blind. It was a disguise he had adopted so that no one would suspect him. I knew it was him."

"But what about the scars on his chest, those mutilated eyes...We had seen them when the auditorium was inaugurated."

Amar prodded the top of Aurangzeb's *firhan,* pulling it lower, revealing the chest. There were no scars there. The partly open eyes too showed no signs of injury, "The scars on his chest and eyes were probably the handiwork of his friend, Dr. Mirwaiz. There were no pellet wounds; it was only cosmetic make up."

"But how did you know it was him?"

"I must say, he played the part of a blind man well. He fooled all of us. But when I went to Abdullah's shop where he was manning the counter, he lifted his hand to get the biscuits from the top shelf. His *firhan* sleeve slipped and I saw his elbow." He yanked up the *firhan* to reveal blackened elbows, heavily calloused, on both hands. He pulled up his sleeves and revealed his own elbows. They too were red and blackened, calloused and coarse. "This happens when you spend long hours lying on the ground with a rifle in hand. When I saw that, I became suspicious. And then I noticed his shoes. They were worn out with extensive travelling and had red mud on the sides. That mud is only found in the upper reaches of the mountains. That's when I knew he was not blind."

"Abdullah was a sympathizer – whether willingly or by force we don't know. But I knew he was lying about his blind nephew who had suddenly appeared. And when he told me that Iqbal had gone to Jammu for supposedly for treatment, I knew that Aurangzeb was just preparing for the strike and that Abdullah would be helping him. That's why I went to his tea shop to look for them, and thank God I was right."

It was starting to get light and in the early dawn he could see other soldiers running towards them. It had stopped snowing now, but it still lay in small white clumps dotting the ground. A faint mist was forming and the mountains in the distance were shrouded in fog. From the direction of the town mosque, he could hear the muezzin's call to the faithful and see the faint bustling as a new day began. He picked up Aurangzeb's rifle from the ground and slung it across his other shoulder. Then he reached out for Shazia, held her gently and then guided her towards the approaching soldiers and safety.